THE OLD IRISH WORLD

BY

ALICE STOPFORD GREEN

PREFACE

Some Irish friends have asked me to print certain lectures concerning Ireland to which they had listened with indulgence; and to reprint also former papers in a manner more convenient for country readers. This volume is the answer to their request. It will be seen that I have not attempted to alter the lectures from their first purpose and form.

The various studies, thus accidentally united, have a connecting link in such evidences as they may contain of civilisation in the old Irish world. A hundred years ago, in 1821, Dr. Petrie noted that while the historians of ancient native origin were unable in their poverty and degradation to pursue the laborious study of antiquities, there were others of a different class and origin who had taken up the subject to bring it into contempt; and these indeed succeeded in the cause for which they, unworthily, laboured. Forty years later he recognised the same influences at work. It would appear, he said in a letter written to Lord Dunraven shortly before his death in 1865, to be considered derogatory to the feeling of superiority in the English mind to accept the belief that Celts of Ireland or Scotland could have been equal, not to say superior in civilisation to their more potent conquerors, or that they could have known the arts of civilised life till these were taught them by the Anglo-Normans. After the lapse of half a century we can still trace the same spirit—so powerful have been the hindrances to serious and impartial enquiry—so slow has been the decline of racial prejudice and political complacency. But in these latter days a great change has silently passed over the peoples. The difficulties of historical research and instruction do indeed remain as great as ever; but in the new society which we see shaping itself in Ireland on natural and no longer on purely artificial lines, there is no reason to fear truth as dangerous or to neglect it as unnecessary. There is now a public ready to be interested not only in Danish and Norman civilisation in Ireland, but also in the Gaelic culture which embraced these and made them its own.

I cannot adequately thank Professor Eoin MacNeill for generously allowing me to embody in my first chapter some of his researches on the history of the Scot wanderings between Scotland and Ireland; it is earnestly to be hoped that he will publish before long the results of his original work.

I owe my warm thanks also to Mr. F. J. Bigger for his unstinted help in references and suggestions out of the stores of his topographical knowledge. I may mention as an instance the grave-stone in Kilclief churchyard carved with a Celtic cross, which he discovered while these pages were going through the press, so that I have been able to note it for the first time among Lecale antiquities.

Mr. R. I. Best has rendered me more services than I can here tell, however gratefully I acknowledge them.

The account of Ardglass has been re-printed with additions, by the kind permission of the Editor of the *Nation*. I have to thank the Editor of the *Nineteenth Century* for leave to add the article on Tradition in History, which is inserted at the request of readers in Ireland.

To prevent mistake I may add a word of explanation that the map, or rather diagram, which is entitled Scandinavian Trade Routes, contains not only those lines of sea-commerce, but also an indication of the ways across Europe which were used by Irish travellers from earlier times. The difference between these routes is clearly indicated in the text.

ALICE STOPFORD GREEN.

April 25, 1912.

THE OLD IRISH WORLD

CHAPTER I

THE WAY OF HISTORY IN IRELAND

IN all the countries of Europe the study of history for a citizen of the State is taken for granted, as the study of tides and currents might be held necessary for a mariner, or of the winds for an air-man, or that of the map for a merchant. It is only a dozen years ago, however, that its study was made compulsory in elementary schools in England, and in that country men are still discussing, by way of lectures and so forth, "What is the Use of History." The historical instinct among the English people has indeed never been very keen, so that, as learned men tell us, it would be more difficult to form a folk-museum in England than in any other country, so few are the objects of a distinctly national character that have survived. The past is rapidly overlaid among men who live intensely in the present and the immediate future. A great gulf separates them from a race like the Irish, to whom the far past and the far future are part of the eternal present, the very condition of thought, the furniture without which the mind is bare.

The Irish, nevertheless, have by long effort been brought under authority to the English mind in history, and an Anglicised Ireland now lies in the wake of England, a laggard in the trough of the wave, rocked by the old commonplaces of the early Victorian age. The hope that our people may win out of that trough lies to a great extent in the new sails set by the National University, if they may at last catch the fresh breezes of Heaven, and be swept into the open sea of free knowledge and candid thinking. In Ireland, as in England, history has been made compulsory in a sense—a sense, we might irreverently say, of the "United Kingdom." It has been made a department of English Grammar, and has further been portioned out to Irishmen as a fragment of English history, strictly confined within dates fixed for that history in the schools of England.

The Irish story is thus shut up as it were like criminals of old in the Tower prison of Little Ease—a narrow place where no man could stand or lie at length. And Irishmen are still driven to discuss in belated fashion the question that all Europe settled long ago—Why should we make the History of our country our serious study?

The reason of Nature for this study is indeed as profound as the being of man. There is no other creature on this planet that can create a history of its kind. To man alone belongs the faculty of looking “before and after,” and considering the story of his race from the first human being that walked the earth. Our first forefather brought with him something new—the power to store up and to celebrate memories of the great dead. His elemental pieties have become part of the whole tradition of our humanity; and that history which he began, and to which we add day by day, is our witness to the separateness of man from the other creatures of this world. When we cherish this study we are proclaiming our pre-eminence among all the living beings that we know. When we let this history fall from us we are sinking to the level of the dumb beasts. As living men, therefore, “let us enjoy, whenever we have an opportunity, the delight of admiration, and perform the duties of reverence.”

There is a practical reason, too, for the knowledge of history. The individual man left to himself is helpless to stand against the powers of the world. Alone he can do nothing. His strength lies in the generations and associations of man behind him, linked by an endless tradition, who have made for him his art, religion, science, politics, social laws. It is only in communion with that company of workers that he can take a step forward. The soul of a country is bound up with the heroes who still

"... people the steep rocks and river banks,
Her natural sanctuaries, with a local soul,
Of independence and stern liberty.”

Rulers and commanders have known this well. When they have wanted to exalt peoples or armies under them, they have opened out to them the glories of their history, and called on them to admit into their souls the spirit of their fathers.

"Up! up! and drink the spirit breathed
From dead men to their kind."

When they have wished to depress and subjugate a race they have slammed the doors of their history on them, and left them alone, spiritless and forlorn, passed by and forgotten by the Ages, despised of themselves and of their neighbours.

Whether therefore as men of a reasonable nature, or as members of a nation, we are bound to make History our all-important study. There is no question about this in any self-respecting nation in Europe. How does the case stand with us in Ireland?

When I first began the study of Irish History, I was dissuaded from it by a man of exceedingly acute mind and wide reading. His argument, I imagine, is a common one, and shows the kind of scruples that are set to bar our way to Irish history—as some primeval race once planted the slope of Cahir Mor on Aran with a forest of jagged standing-stones, to forbid all entrance to the fortress uplifted there above the expanse of the Ocean in its freedom. Why, said my typical objector, should we turn away from the great highways of the world's progress, with their sweeping procession of Empires and great Dominions, to lose ourselves in the maze where humble and unsuccessful nationalities walk obscurely. Stimulate the spirit of young men by giving them the examples of heroes whose fame has sounded through the earth, and societies that have been adorned by triumph. Let the men of local fame, the guardians of smaller nationalities, rest in darkness, and let us follow the sun in its strength.

We may remember one of the snares laid by the Prince of Evil for the Son of Man, when he set Him on a high place above the kingdoms of the world, to bend His soul before their ostentatious glory. From the mountain Satan displayed the emblems of their pride, palaces and towers and treasuries, "knowing that it was by those alone that he himself could have been so utterly lost to rectitude and beatitude. Our Saviour spurned the temptation, and the greatest of His miracles was accomplished." England was just at the outset of her imperial career when Milton, in his "Paradise Regained," pictured that tremendous scene, the passing of the empires in their state before the judgment of the Divine Reason. The prodigious procession was marshalled from the very dawn of history, powers and dominions sweeping over the earth, and disappearing with the suddenness with which they rose. Not one has survived. In the shifting scene forms of states move and stir dimly like the fallen angels from "Paradise Lost" as they lay prone, extended on the flood of ruin and combustion. One scheme of government after another is lifted up to be cast down—tyranny, oligarchy, slavery, commercialism, communism, parliaments, theocracies. The great warriors and the great statesmen are alike entombed in the ruins of their empires. "Head and crown drop together, and are overlooked." On the other hand, when empires have fallen, the nationalities have not always perished. They die only with the utter extermination of the people. So long as the old stock lingers on the soil, there is a spirit that can outlive all empires, form the scourge of conquerors, and set the last barrier to pride of dominion. We know how peoples enclosed within small states, fed from deep sources of heritage and tradition, have given the impress of their local passion to their art. Out of the intensity of national life have come those high inspirations that have given to us all that is best of literature, poetry, painting, sculpture, music, and however deeply the artist has felt the influence of the world outside, his ultimate power lies in the spirit which has entered into him from his native state and the race of which he sprang. The generous influences of local patriotism were recognised by the greatest political thinker that modern Ireland has sent out: "To be attached," said Burke, "to the sub-division, to love the little platoon we belong to in society, is the first principle (the germ as it were) of public affections."

Perhaps, we might also suggest to our objector, the lesser nationalities are even now, in these days of triumphant Imperialism, beginning to have their revenge. The study of small societies seems to become fashionable among the new reformers. Do we not hear from all sides of the education, discipline, and public spirit of countries compassed within bounds suited to man's apprehension? With what respect do not Unionists extol the industrial success of States such as Holland and Denmark, for example. Even now do we not hear English Imperialists crying out that perhaps Switzerland has got the secret of the democratic mind, or Norway, or New South Wales, or Arizona; might not England take a lesson from some little self-contained and thrifty community on the use of the referendum? It would seem that the influence of small commonwealths is not yet extinct among us.

It is very certain that Ireland of all countries, if left to itself, would never of its own will allow history to lie in a backwater among the flotsam of the current. History was the early study of the Irish, the inspiration of their poets and writers. Every tribesman of old knew, not only the great deeds and the famous places of his own clan, but of the whole of Ireland. In the lowliest cabin the songs of Irish poets lived on for hundreds of years, and dying fathers left to sons as their chief inheritance the story of their race. When war, poverty, the oppression of the stranger, hindered the printing of Irish records, there was not a territory in all Ireland that did not give men to make copies of them, hundreds of thousands of pages, over and over again, finely written after the manner of their fathers. Through centuries of suffering down to within living memory the long procession of scribes was never broken, men tilling small farms, labouring in the fields, working at a blacksmith's forge. And this among a people of whom Burke records that in two hundred thousand houses for their exceeding poverty a candle, on which a tax lay, was never lighted. As we follow the lines and count the pages of such manuscripts, we see the miracle of the passion in these men's hearts. No relics in Ireland are more touching than these volumes, and none should be more reverently collected and preserved. They form a singular treasure such as no country in all Europe possesses.

But now, in spite of this tradition, history is more backward in Ireland than in any other country. Here alone there is a public opinion which resents its being freely written, and there is an opinion, public or official, I scarcely know which to call it, which prevents its being freely taught. And between the two, history has a hard fight for life.

Take the question of writing. History may conceivably be treated as a science. Or it may be interpreted as a majestic natural drama or poem. Either way has much to be said for it. Both ways have been nobly attempted in other countries. But neither of these courses is thought of in Ireland. Here history has a peculiar doom. It is enslaved in the chains of the Moral Tale—the good man (English) who prospered, and the bad man (Irish) who came to a shocking end—the kind of ethical formula which, for all our tutors and teachers could do, never deceived the generosity of childhood. The good man in the moral tale of Ireland is not even a fiction of Philosophy or of History. He is, oddly enough, the offspring of Grammar alone, and carries the traces of his dry and uninspired pedigree. He owes his being, in fact, to the English dislike for a foreign language. The Gael, as we know, ever faithful to the tradition of his race, while he sang and recited and wrote and copied his story with an undying passion, did these things in his own speech. The Norman or "Frank" settlers, true "citizens of the world," adopted his tongue, his poetry, and his patriotic enthusiasm. When the English arrived, however, they according to their constant insular tradition refused to learn a strange language, so that the only history of Ireland they could discern was that part of it which was written in English—that is, the history of the English colonists told by themselves. On this contracted record they have worked with industry and self-congratulation. They have laid down the lines of a story in which the historian's view is constantly fixed on England. All that the Irish had to tell of themselves remained obscured in an unknown tongue. The story of the whole Irish population thus came to be looked on as merely a murky prelude to the civilizing work of England—a preface savage, transitory, and of no permanent interest, to be rapidly passed over till we come to the English pages of the book. Thus two separate stories went on side by side. The Irish did not know the language which held the legend of English virtue and consequent wealth. The English could not translate the subterranean legend of Irish poetry, passion, and fidelity. Religion added new distinctions. Virtues were Protestant, the sins of the prodigal were Catholic. Finally, class feeling had its word. The upper class went to their university, and their manners and caste instincts entitled them as of course to the entire credence of their own social world; the lower class were alleged to be men whose manners were common and their prejudices vulgar.

In this way there grew up an orthodox history based on sources in the English tongue alone. The Colonists laid down by authority its dogmas and axioms. All that agreed with this conventional history was reputed serious and scholarly: whatever diverged from it was partial, partizan, or prejudiced. "Impartiality" and "loyalty" became technical terms, with a special meaning for Ireland. The two words were held also to be interchangeable. A strictly "impartial" writer must not let his "loyal" eye swerve from the fixed point, England. As a judicious Englishman said of his compatriots, they only think a man impartial when he has gone over to the opposite side.

The results of this system are conspicuous. A Frenchman may unreproved write with affection and ardour of France, and an Englishman of England. An Irishman, however, is in another case. He must have no patriotic fire for his own people. He must not acclaim their victories nor mourn their defeats. Take an illustration of this temper. A clergyman has lately written to the *Church of Ireland Gazette* to condemn history readers "written from an anti-English and anti-Church point of view"; he complains that the writer describes the battle of the Blackwater in 1598, where the English were routed, as "a glorious victory for the O'Neill." Such a phrase as this cannot be allowed to Irishmen. Or as a writer to the *Irish Times* puts a similar argument: "If the Nationalists want for ever to live in the glories of the past and to harp upon them, why do they not go far enough back ... to the time when they ate their grandmothers ... and indulged in all sorts of hellish rites."

In fact, as we trudge along the dull beaten road of the orthodox history we never escape, not for a moment, from the monotonous running commentary which sounds continually at our side. "Nomadic," "primitive," "wigwam," "aboriginal," "savage," "barbarous," "lawless"—the words are always at hand. In the moral tale the accustomed stream of precept and delation never runs dry. It follows us through all the strictly "impartial" writers. The Irishman was a "kerne." The Irish word cethern (kerne) meaning a troop or company of soldiers, probably foot soldiers, is as old as theLatin *caterva* with which it is cognate, or the Umbrian *kateramu*, and so is of quite respectable lineage; but being a foreign word to the Englishman, he used it as a natural term of contempt, as though a Chinese should cry "sailor" or "merchant" when he meant to say "English devil." More than that, the Irishman was a "nomad," apparently because he sent his cattle to graze on the hills in summer—a custom which in modern Switzerland is held to be quite respectable by admirers of Federalism. This "nomad" idea is familiarly handed about from one writer to another. One of the most esteemed historians in Dublin was Mr. Litton Falkiner, who has added some notable pages to later Anglo-Irish history. Yet he was satisfied to dismiss the Irish population of mediæval times in one terse phrase: "the pastoral, and in great measure nomadic Celts, who stood for the Irish people before the 12th century"—in other words, before the Norman invasion. This absurd sentence seems to pass current; no objection has been made to it. What would educated Englishmen think of a leading historian who dismissed the pre-Norman population of that island as "boorish Low-Dutch, hut-dwellers round a common field cut into strips after their barbarous manner, *who stood for the English people before the Norman Conquest*?" Trivialities and ignorances of this sort are not in fashion in English history, and it is time that they were out of fashion in Ireland.

Irishmen of the north still preserved, Mr. Falkiner told us, even to the end of the 17th century, "all the primitive characteristics of the scarcely more than nomadic civilisation of Ulster." With summary contempt he pretended to dispose of what he fancifully termed "the lawless banditti who commonly formed the body-guard of an Irish chief"; and in the orthodox manner confronts "Irish law" and "Irish lawlessness" under what he called "the English ownership of Ireland." The great Hugh of Tyrone is described as looking "on the onward march of English institutions with feelings not very different from those with which the aborigines of the American continent beheld the advance of the stranger from the east." In the same spirit he informed Englishmen that Ireland was sadly deficient in the wealth of historical and literary associations which form the romantic charm of England. "Cathedral cities, in the sense in which the term is understood in England, Ireland may be almost said to be without. A few of the towns," he generously admitted, "contain, indeed, the remains of ecclesiastical and monastic buildings. But even where these exist they are, with one or two exceptions, sadly deficient in human interest." It is a cheap method, even if it is one out of date elsewhere, to deny human interest to a subject which one has learned to ignore, and may desire to see forgotten. Can no human interest touch the heart in Dromahair or Donegal or Glendalough? There is a remote and little-known road in the plains of Mayo where a singular sight may be seen. Near it stand the ruins of a majestic abbey founded over seven hundred years ago (1189-1190), by Cathal O'Connor (whose foster-father's tomb has lately been found at Knockmoy with its Irish inscription). Nave and transepts were laid bare and open from their immense gable ends, and the tower flung from the four splendid arches that supported it, but the old vaulted roof of the choir still remains; and here, it is said, in this remoteness, is the only ancient church of the Irish where, amid the universal destruction and confiscation, they have been able to carry on their old worship from the old days till now. In this land of the banished—"to hell or Connacht"—mass was without ceasing celebrated in the choir; and from the hearts of the worshippers kneeling in the nave and transepts under the open sky a prophecy arose that when the church was roofed once more Ireland would be freed. Songs still sung among Connacht peasants tell of such services amid ruins of their holy places, the priests wet with the rain, the women's clothes bedraggled, the men carrying small stone flags so as to have a dry spot for their knees. Not in any way was such a place like an English cathedral, but if brave men's vows and prayers and tears for seven centuries can confer human interest the stones of Ballintober are precious.

The problem remains, however (for insoluble problems beset every false position) that according to Mr. Falkiner's theory the history of towns and cathedrals only began with "the English ownership." How was it that these Englishmen left none of their "romantic charm" there? What strange history lies hidden behind this saying?

Another historian takes up the same taunt—a true scholar and worker who has added to our knowledge of the close of Stuart rule in Ireland. "The Irish," says Dr. Murray, "are indeed a strange race.... No monument marks the site where the Irish hero and the Irish thinker repose.... The graves of a patriot like Owen Roe O'Neill, and of a statesman like Archbishop King ... are unknown. The thrill that an Englishman feels in Westminster Abbey when he enters the presence of the mighty dead is denied an Irishman, for he has not taken care of the dust of his immortals." A memorial by the defeated Irish to Archbishop King of Dublin, ardent supporter of the Dutch conqueror, passionate worker for the Protestant succession, four times Lord Justice for the government of Ireland under William in those days of agony and despair—this is a lofty counsel of perfection, such as we give to others. The Irish raised no monument to Owen Roe O'Neill—no monument, with Cromwell's soldiers abroad in the land, to the general proclaimed by the English Government "traitor, rebel, disturber of the common peace"—is that the charge? Alas! I wonder from that day to this what welcome would have been given in a Protestant churchyard, guarded by the conquerors, to an Irish memorial over the grave of Owen Roe O'Neill. The dust of the Irish immortals lies indeed far scattered. Has Dr. Murray ever stood in the solitary burial places of Rath Croghan, of Iniscaltra, of Clonmacnois? Has he counted the stones in Athenry or those heaped up in Burris? Has he seen the bones of the martyrs strewn from sea to sea? Surely he himself has told us that "the Irish custom of burying their dead in an old ruined church or monastery was forbidden," and that not by the Irish, but by the Church of the English. From the Reformation until eighty-two years ago every Irish Catholic was needs carried at death to a Protestant cemetery, and it is only within the life-time of men now living that, when Catholic prayers at the grave were denied, the Irish people at last secured in 1829 a burying place of their own.

This fiction of a "strange race" has become a kind of special philosophy which is dragged in to interpret the most ordinary actions of the Irish. For example, "the march of the soldiery upset the balance of the excitable Irish farmer, and he neglected his land"—a fact which in any other country would need no "race" explanation. Through the story of that war, whose end was to transfer the soil of Ireland, five-sixths of it, to lords of another race and religion, the old inhabitants of two thousand years' possession are made to appear as "the Irish factions"; their vice is patent, while English crimes are accidental, inadvertent, or high-spirited. If we want to know why the Irish people lost faith in the Stuarts who had betrayed and outraged them at every turn, we are referred to the simple habits of a strange and childish race. "The Celt wants to see a sovereign regularly in order to adore him": "A principle must be set forth by a person, and the more attractive the person the stronger the hold of the principle." As we watch the strong ceaseless current of Irish life such theories are swept beyond our sight. The Irish poet told his people another tale:

"It is the coming of King James that took Ireland from us,
With his one shoe English and his one shoe Irish
He would neither strike a blow nor would he come to terms,
And that has left, so long as they shall exist, misfortune upon the Gaels."

In his laborious work on the Norman settlement, Mr. Orpen deals with the Irish in the usual conventional manner:—"The members of this family were always killing one another." "The chieftain ... had no higher conception of duty than to increase the power of his clan; with this object in view, he was stayed by no scruples"; as for the clansman, "the sentiment for 'country' in any sense more extended than that of his own tribal territory, was alike to him and to his chief unknown." This description, like the terms "tribal" and "nomad," has long been habitual, and accepted with as little enquiry as those words. Mr. Orpen's clients, the "Normans," we may assume to have been nobly free from any such barbarous notions of individual aggrandisement, regardless of "their country's" claims.

Mr. Bagwell, the leading historian of the English occupation under Tudors and Stuarts, throws his searchlight on the Irish:—"They were barbarous, but they could appreciate virtue." "The Irish were subtle, fond of license, and ready for anything as long as it was not for their good." May we remember the saying of the Irish themselves in those days:—"Ask for nothing that you would not deem a benefit to you, and before all praise God." Again, according to Mr. Bagwell, "the people had no other idea of trade than to extort exorbitant prices." This quality scarcely seems to need a racial explanation; it has been found elsewhere in time of war. But under all circumstances the "primeval" theory of Irishmen must be maintained. The character of the "natives"—using this word with its "savage" implication—plays a great part in our history. Thus, when a boat load of treasure from the Armada was washed on shore Mr. Bagwell notes that "such unaccustomed wares as velvet and cloth of gold, fell into the hands of the natives." Cloth of gold and velvet had for centuries been known to the wealthy Irish; even in England they were not the clothing of the "natives," if such a term could be applied to Englishmen. Again we are told that "the Irish, by being held always at arm's length, had become more Irish and less civilised than ever"; *held at arm's length* is an ingenious phrase for evicting a people from their homes, and throwing them out on bogs and mountains. The hardships of hunted famine-stricken outlaws hanging round their old homes, is represented in this kind of history as the life which would be naturally chosen by wild Irish "nomads." "True children of the mist, they O'Tooles] either bivouacked in the open or crept into wretched huts to which Englishmen hesitated to give the name of houses. They cultivated no land." "Thus one by one did the chiefs of tribal Ireland devour each other." As for "the men of free blood, whose business had always been fighting, and who would never work ... when the chiefs were gone they had nothing to do but to plunder, or to live at the expense of their more industrious, but less noble, neighbours." "The island was poor and the people barbarous, and no revenue could be expected." It is true, indeed, that the wealth did not go the way of the Crown; officials had other uses for it.

In the same way Mr. Chart, in his study of Irish life during the dark years after the Union—years of acute suffering, hunger, disillusionment and despair—discovers "a sullen discontent which, as usually happens in Ireland, broke out occasionally into acts of lawlessness and barbarity," as if some special form of iniquity had its home in Ireland. At a time when the whole people in England were in a turmoil of revolt, on the verge of revolution, he mourns "the fatal Irish tendency to rush into extremes," and that magistrates and police had to accustom "a hot-headed and violent-tempered race to curb itself within legal limits"—as if this was an unusual fact, peculiar to this one race of the world, predestinate to evil. It would seem that in Ireland alone it is not safe to give any man "full and unconstrained control over his personal and political enemies," and therefore "Ireland is no country for a volunteer police."

I suppose there is not another history in the world in which this free slinging of blame and advice is continuously kept up at so fine a pitch. If a problem in Irish life lifts its head, some puzzling fact or tendency that demands explanation, a stone is ready in the orthodox historian's sling: the dilemma is ended by one of the useful words—"primitive," "tribal," "kerne," "nomad," "barbarous," "Celtic." By constant reiteration I fancy writer and reader now scarcely notice them, so much have they become the symbols of Irish history, and so deeply have they sunk into the public mind.

Thus the stream of calumny still flows on. The latest voice from Trinity College, that of Professor Mahaffy, in his Introduction to the third volume of the "Georgian Society," is of the old familiar type. It should be, he explains, "the interest and duty" of historians to maintain certain desirable opinions—this, according to Dr. Mahaffy, adds to their credibility. Once more, therefore, we have from him "the elements of primeval savagery which still existed in the Irish people, and which they had in common with almost all primitive races and societies" (and this by the way, in the 18th century, after six hundred years of English compulsion). How well we know the old battered and time-exhausted phrase! Of course we have again our old friend, the story of O'Cahan sitting with the naked women, served up as the ever-repeated type of all the generations of Irish in their habitual squalor. For, we are told, "since the earliest times the greater part of the Irish ... have not found any discomfort in squalor." But for English law this singular people would apparently never put on clothes at all, winter or summer, good or bad weather, in any northern gale from the Arctic ice. Ulstermen now-a-days are certainly a degenerate race in physical endurance.

It is interesting to follow this story of O'Cahan.

The story begins with a Bohemian baron, name unknown, whom Foynes Moryson, an Englishman, saw on one occasion. Here is the exact tale: —"The foresaid Bohemian baron, coming out of Scotland to us by the north parts of the wild Irish, told me in great earnestness (when I attended him at the Lord Deputy's command), that he coming to the house of the O'Cane, a great lord among them, was met at the door with sixteen women, all naked, excepting their loose mantles; whereof eight or ten were very fair, and two seemed very nymphs; with which strange sight his eyes being dazzled, they led him into the house, and there sitting down by the fire with crossed legs like tailors, and so low as could not but offend chaste eyes, desired him to sit down with them. Soon after O'Kane, the lord of the country, came in all naked excepting a loose mantle and shoes, which he put off as soon as he came in, and entertaining the baron after his best manner in the Latin tongue, desired him to put off his apparel, which he thought to be a burden to him, and to sit naked by the fire with his naked company."

Now on this tale let me make two or three remarks.

We may ask, in the first place, why this one story is repeated on every occasion by historians of what I might call the "savage" type; why, omitting all other accounts, it is singled out as the typical instance of daily life in Ireland. Is this one of the views which, according to Dr. Mahaffy, it should be "the interest and duty" of impartial and loyal historians to maintain?

The story originated with a "Bohemian baron," of whom we know nothing; it was reported by the English secretary of Mountjoy, whom he praises for the number of "rebels" he had "brought to their last home"; to both of them the Irish were nothing more than savages of a low type. We may remember that this is the only story of the kind cited from Ulster. A Spanish captain, escaped from the Armada, travelled through Connacht and Ulster and the O'Cahan country for several months of hiding from English soldiers; he too talked Latin in the many Irish houses which gave him shelter, but in the book of his wanderings there is no such incident as this.

There would seem to be need of some strictness of enquiry—some caution in discussing the tale. At the best the outlines of the baron's story are vague. What decorations he himself may have introduced into it, and what further ornaments Fynes Moryson may have added, we do not know. We may, perhaps, judge by the embellishments which later writers have introduced. It is possible that the baron and the secretary, not inferior to their successors in contempt of the Irish, may have equalled them also in literary skill and the gift of embroidering a narrative. Let us see, therefore, some of these decorations.

Froude takes up the tale:—"If Fynes Moryson may be believed, the daughters of distinguished Ulster chiefs squatted on the pavement round the hall fires of their father's castles, in the presence of strangers, as bare of clothing as if Adam had never sinned." Here we see the "women," who, for all the original story has to tell us, might be servants, dependants, or refugees gathered in from the war and pillage by which O'Cahan's country was then ravaged, are transformed into "daughters of chiefs," the "house" turns into "pavements" by the "hall-fires of castles," and the incident has become a universal custom.

Then Professor Mahaffy arrives with a series of versions. "O'Cahan, though living in a hovel, could speak Latin." More particularly, it was a shantie of mud and wattles, without rafters, and the cattle and swine occupied the same room as the masters; so he explains in a lecture on "Elizabethan Ireland." A more circumstantial account appears in "An Epoch in Irish History." In this the traveller is received by the "ladies of the chieftain's household." "They brought him into the thatched cabin which was their residence," and throwing off their mantles invited him to do likewise before the chief came in—an invitation which the unknown "women" of the baron's tale did not give. The baron's "house" has already changed into castles with pavements, then into a hovel, and a thatched cabin, but the picture of savagery is not yet lurid enough, and there is a further transformation which, possibly from its supposed importance, is dragged into a description of society in the Dublin Georgian houses of the 18th century. "The O'Cahan in his wigwam, surrounded by his stark naked wives (why not squaws?) and daughters, addressed the astonished foreign visitor in fluent Latin." The "wigwam" and the "wives" show the unimpaired fertility of Professor Mahaffy's imagination. His pronouncements, the *Irish Times* assures us of this essay, "carry historical value of the highest degree." It will be interesting to watch his further adornments of his favourite tale. It will also be interesting to see how long professors of Trinity College will still invite Irish students to enter there by offering this curious bait of conventional insults to their race and country, and new varieties of old slanders.

We might remember the scene in Galway a few years later, where high-born ladies, plundered of all their property by the rapacious soldiers, sinking with shame before the gaze of the public in their ragged clothes, covered themselves with embroidered table-covers, or a strip of tapestry taken from the walls, or lappets cut from the bed-curtains, or with blankets, sheets, or table-cloths. "You would have taken your oath," says the contemporary writer, "that all Galway was a masquerade, the unrivalled home of scenic buffoons, so irresistibly ludicrous were the varied dresses of the poor women." Why do not the Colonial historians give this scene as showing the habitual taste and pleasure of the Galway ladies?

Dr. Mahaffy has some other lights to throw on Irish history. "The contempt for traders as such ... is," he says, "like all such prejudice in Ireland, the survival of the contempt which the meanest members of any Irish clan felt for any profession save that of arms, and the preying on the churl." The despisers of trade whom he is describing in this passage are the English landowners of the Williamite settlement, who had finally ousted the Irish from their lands, and taken them over as Protestant Englishmen, men of "a better race." This conquering class naturally felt a contempt for their victims, the evicted Catholic Irish, who were allowed for the benefit of their lords and rulers to plough and to trade, while deprived of civil and social rights. But I do not know how those lordly squires would like to have heard that they represented the prejudices of "the meanest member of an Irish clan," accustomed to prey on "the churl," whoever he was. As for the Irish clansman who is supposed to look on traders as outcasts, he appears to be a fiction of the essayist's fancy. Where in Irish records will proofs be found of contempt for a trader? Their story seems to be quite the other way. It may be convenient, however, for the defaming of the Irish to despise and ignore those records. Moreover, since Irish abbeys and cathedrals have been pronounced by Mr. Litton Falkiner not to be like the English ones, why need an Irish writer stoop into their ruins to seek out the story written there? No, it is easier to keep the slander running, to swell its volume, and to increase its violence. Yet in those ruins any man who will may look upon the countless tombs of Irishmen who (so long as the conqueror's law allowed their desolate companies to enter the ancient shrines) were borne by their friends to rest in the roofless nave or before the high altar under great slabs with the signs of their trade, the tailor's instruments, the carpenter's tools, and the mason's, the labourer's plough, and the trader's ship, deeply graven beside their names—no emblems of shame in those last sanctuaries of the Irish people.

Social life in Ireland, through all the ages, Dr. Mahaffy describes as especially immoral. The young girls, he says, were generally accessible to the squire and his sons all through Irish history, and suffered no disgrace, but married all the better for such an adventure. "All through Irish history" is a liberal and characteristic phrase to use of English squires and their sons. The tradition of absolute landlord power still lives in the Irish country-side, when girls were told the price at which they might save their family from being driven out of the home held by their ancestors for hundreds of years, and left to die on the roadside of hunger, or in the coffin-ship of plague. With security of tenure for the Irish poor such ordeals have passed into history. As for reports of English tourists, they resemble the travellers' tales which everywhere and at all times various countries have heard on the manners of their neighbours. It is well to remember Gibbon's reflection on general charges of this sort. Manuel, Emperor of the East, visited England in 1400, and coming from Constantinople was shocked at English conduct:—"The most singular circumstance of their manners," he reported, "is their disregard of conjugal honour and of female chastity. In their mutual visits, as the first act of hospitality, the guest is welcomed in the embraces of their wives and daughters; among friends they are lent and borrowed without shame; nor are the islanders offended at this strange commerce." "We may smile at the credulity, or resent the injustice of the Greek," Gibbon reflects, "but his credulity and injustice may teach an important lesson; to distrust the accounts of foreign and remote nations, and to suspend our belief of every tale that deviates from the laws of nature and the character of man."

English writers have forgotten a grave disadvantage to themselves in the moral tale of the good and bad man (besides its incredibility and its dullness). In this version of Irish history the Englishman's triumph remains a poor thing, destitute of interest or value, where the fame of the victor is abased and confounded by the worthlessness of his foe. The Irish warriors are mostly described as drunkards, cowards, and barbarians. Dr. Mahaffy likens Shane O'Neill to a Moor or a Zulu. Hugh of Tyrone "was a polished courtier on the surface, with a barbarous core." Here is Mr. Bagwell's portrait of Shane, whose organisation and defence of Ulster cost Elizabeth over £147,000 of English money (in modern money probably over £1,500,000) without counting the enormous cesses laid on the country, and three thousand five hundred of her soldiers slain. "He is said to have been a glutton, and was certainly a drunkard." The story of drunkenness seems to have originated in his mud-baths, such as are now commonly ordered for rheumatism. Once started, the fable was persistent. "That drunken brain was, nevertheless, clear enough to baffle Elizabeth for a long time." His conduct of a war which cost Elizabeth so much is described:—"Shane, who had been indulging as usual in wine or whisky, came up at the moment." "Shane, who was never remarkable for dashing courage, retired into the wood." "Shane, whose reputation for courage is not high, slipped out at the back of his tent." So, I believe, did de Wet, instead of waiting to be killed. At the last, "the love of liquor probably caused his death"; here indeed Mr. Bagwell contradicts the Lord Deputy Sidney himself, who boasts that Shane was tricked and murdered by a Scotsman in Sidney's pay, the last of a series of attempts at assassination. From the point of view that "barbarians" are usually childish, Mr. Bagwell tells how the important chiefs, MacWilliam Burke and MacGillapatrick, were given titles and robes of Earl and Baron, "in the belief that titles and little acts of civility would weigh more with these rude men than a display of force." He complains that the best-laid English military plans of occupation of this country, instead of proceeding without interruption from the natives, might be "frustrated by one of those unexpected acts of treachery in which Irish history abounds." However, even in treachery the Irish were incompetent. "Irish plots are commonly woven in sand." "In this, as in so many other Irish insurrections, there was no want of double traitors; of men who had neither the constancy to remain loyal, nor the courage to persevere in rebellion."

With such a rabble we can only wonder that there was any need of an English army at all; or how the conflict could last a year (not to say a few hundreds of them); or why England should have sent over her very best generals, her stoutest governors, and a prodigious deal of her gold. It was the bogs, apparently, that swallowed up those inconceivable hosts and coins.

Under the "savage" theory military matters lose all interest; but they are given to us with pitiless detail. Expeditions of soldiers against famine-stricken peasants without arms, raids of mere slaughter, the chasing of outlaws from a lake island, are described with the minuteness of a genuine campaign. These things, no doubt, are in the books. There are plenty of reports from officials, very humanly anxious to justify themselves or to magnify their feats. But history after all claims some revising power, and we need another standard of proportion than the vanity of a lieutenant. It is impossible to give vitality to a story in which highly armed and civilised Englishmen are represented as wiping out with cannon and gunpowder a savage and unarmed crowd of peasants—in which honour, courage, and progress are supposed to be eternally confronted with chicanery, barbarity, and treachery. No one wants to hear that tale. Such a history turns to inconceivable tediousness, of no use to any living soul.

Meanwhile vast tracts of history have been set aside as apparently not worth exploring. Where, for example, shall we find a serious account, with the guidance of modern scholarship, of the hundred and fifty years between the battle of Clontarf and the landing of the Norman barons. The people were no longer in the tribal state. The change to a kind of feudalism had come. What was the form of that feudalism? How did it differ from the system that had grown out of other conditions elsewhere? There is not so much as a chapter in any book, or a pamphlet, occupied with the land system of the earlier middle ages, what changes the Norman settlement brought, or what forms of social life did actually exist. The campaign of Edward Bruce is usually said to be a central turning point in Irish history, but who will guide us to any adequate study of it? There are no monographs on Desmonds, O'Neills, O'Donnells, Fitzgeralds, Butlers, Clanrickards, and so on. No annals of the provinces or kingdoms have been compiled, nor chronologies. The work of the two great Earls of Kildare is one of the most critical periods of Irish history: it still awaits a historian. Who has examined the history of the schools and education? Who has worked out the industrial development? How can we learn what were the negotiations by which Henry VIII. carried the claim to be King of Ireland? Here are fields too long deserted waiting for workers. Here are a few of the immense voids, into which our writers fling, like bundles of dried straw, their vain words—"savage," "primeval," "lawless," "brutish," and the rest. In the history of Ireland nothing has been completed. That which is unknown disturbs, and may overturn the vulgar conclusions from the fragments known. We are for ever walking through a country unmapped. To be sure it is full of sign-posts put up at hazard—"To English Civilisation." Where every road is marked to lead to the same inn, why should travellers discuss, debate, and ask questions? What reason can there be to loiter by the way? The English fingerpost is always there.

Some day perhaps the Irish race in this island will no longer seem to lie beyond the need, and below the honour, of the historical method. Ireland will have a history like other nations. It is possible to conceive that out of its peoples, English or Irish, there may arise some great thinker or poet who will set before us the two civilizations that have met here; in other words, the efforts by which two highly endowed races endeavoured to solve the problem that has perplexed every people that has ever yet appeared in this world—how to shape a community where men may live in safety, freedom, and happiness. The Celts had waged the fight for their civilization to the walls of Rome itself. They had left the valleys of the Danube and the Rhine and the plains of Gaul red with their blood. Now, on the outermost border of the world their last conflict awaited them. Within the mountain rim of Ireland, with silent Nature to keep the lists, two peoples met to fight out the last issues on that fatal soil. Here, imprisoned by the Ocean, the antagonists stood for centuries to their battle: every passion exalted, the splendours of courage, the majesty of despair, all skill of surprises, all glory of chivalry, triumph and sorrow, Christian pieties, and the surging up amid the upheaval of human nature of the mysterious superstitions of elemental man, and of his ferocities. What affections of race lay behind such a struggle? What was its meaning? What of beauty, of happiness, or of virtue did each civilization in fact offer to man? What was gained, what was lost? Here would have been a history of fire and flame, a new outlook on the fate of commonwealths, a theme worthy of an English or an Irish patriot.

In the long task of giving its true balance to the history of Ireland, by the discovery of all the facts, and the adjudging of their place, controversy will be lively. Every Irishman for certain will be ready for a battle of wits. But let us keep our intelligence perfectly clear on one point. We shall hear a great deal of "impartiality" and a "judicial mind." Here we must make no mistake. Impartiality of intellect need not mean insensibility of heart. Let us suppose that the intellect should have no pre-possession at all, not even in favour of English civilization, nor of the idol of the market-place, "the Wealth of Nations"—its delicate balance should drop now on this side, now on that, without a shadow of prejudice or a hint of obstinacy, abhorrent of convention, with never a predilection. But impartiality of the heart—that is another matter. Who will pretend to comprehend human life who has no great affection of the soul? The generous heart knows no balancing hesitation between the man who deserts his country and the man who defends it; he alone can interpret the hero in whose soul some answering passion flames; and I suppose that the understanding of a commonwealth will best come to him who is most responsive to a variety of human emotions. I think we could do with a change of partialities in Ireland—fewer orthodox predilections of the head, if it might be so, and some illumination from the heart.

A new examination of Irish history is indeed of the utmost importance to our people. The leading reviews, text-books, and histories in England with one accord have presented Ireland to the English people under the "savage" aspect, and their statements have been too frequently accepted. Hear the common opinion as Tennyson put it: "Kelts are all made furious fools.... They live in a horrible island, and have no history of their own worth the least notice. Could not anyone blow up that horrible island with dynamite and carry it off in pieces—a long way off?" The same gloomy picture is still spread before England. Mr. Fletcher, a Fellow of All Souls, records that "it was quite common to bleed a cow for a refreshing drink of blood," and that "there were no exports save the said cow-skins," though with these the Irish apparently managed to buy "red seas of claret." Shane O'Neill was killed "by his own people whom he was plundering!" Degradation was universal, as we learn from a sentence absolutely amazing in its colossal and unscrupulous ignorance—"though his name had once been FitzNigel or de Burgh, it gradually became

O'Neill or O'Bourke!" Mr. Rudyard Kipling joins Mr. Fletcher in declaring that Irish history "was all broken heads and stolen cows, as it had been for a thousand years," and that Irishmen had no interest or care for their religion till they discovered a use for it as a warcry against England. Accounts of Ireland equally contrary to fact and common sense serve in political controversy. English politicians assert on platforms that Irishmen of themselves had never any national life or duty at all, that the first gleam of true patriotism was taught them by England since the Union, that Ireland had no conception of a Parliament till England gave it to her people, when the boon was so misused and misunderstood by an incompetent race (the English in Ireland, be it remembered) that in the higher interests of man it had to be withdrawn. As for the desire of self-government, "some people said it was a matter of historical sentiment. The humour of it was that there never was a real Irish kingdom at all. The Parliament which it was sought to restore to Ireland was given to it by England. The historical sentiment and loyalty which Mr. John Redmond was talking was the greatest humbug that was ever preached." There are others who argue, Dr. Mahaffy among them, that practically there is not any more a Celtic race in Ireland, but one so mixed in blood that it no longer, if it ever did, contains the materials of a nation. The Celtic people, to their honour, have never denied a national brotherhood to Danes, Normans, English, or Palatines, who loyally entered into the Irish commonwealth. But as to political theories of the vanishing of the race, we have only to examine them by known facts, and turn to the Report of the Registrar-General in 1909 for proof that in the mingling of peoples the Celtic is still the predominant element over all the rest; and if this proof is conclusive, even in the register of merely Irish names, how enormous would be its increased weight if we could reckon in Celtic families the change from Irish names which has gone on ceaselessly since the thirteenth century, and is still constantly occurring at this moment—a change which, however lamentable, cannot alter the blood and the inheritance.

Irishmen are often warned to waste no time in looking back at the past. But if England draws the moral from her interpretation of history, we must learn our lesson too—only it must be a lesson more serious, exact, and worthy of an educated people. We have had experience of how profound and vicious may be the practical effect of a history unscientific, irresponsible, prejudiced, and incomplete. Out of ignorance of the past, what sound policy can grow for the future? I suppose that in civilized Europe, among the speeches on State affairs of prominent statesmen, we could find no parallel to historical verdicts so crude and unsubstantial as those which are given to us by a certain group of political leaders and writers in England, concerning the Irish portion of the "Empire" of which they make their boast. How many are the ignorances and negligences which still do service unreproved among those who claim to be the chief upholders of a "United Kingdom," and exponents of the "Imperial" faith.

In Ireland we have still indeed a heavy road to travel. When history has been written, what about the teaching of it, or the learning, in this country? Who will make the way free for that?

Let me put this matter before you by way of contrast. You have heard the fame of Sparta, the land of heroes who won at the Thermopylæ a far-shining glory that will ever stir the hearts of men. Montaigne reminds us that in the matchless policy of Sparta to build up a noble State, it is worthy of great consideration that the education of the children was the first and principal charge. "And, therefore, was it not strange," he says, "if Antipater requiring fifty of their children for hostages, they answered clean contrary to what we would do, 'that they would rather deliver him twice so many men'; so much did they value and esteem the loss of their country's education." Now in this training up of men to be citizens of the finest quality, the only one book-study absolutely enforced in Sparta was History—to the mockery and contempt of neighbouring Doctors of letters and literature of the time. "Idiots and foolish people," scoffed the high-class Athenian professor, adept in polite languages and fine phrasing and the elegancies of culture, and not neglectful of the profits to be got by professing them; "idiots and foolish people, who only amuse themselves to know the succession of kings, and establishing and declination of estates, and such-like trash of flim-flam tales." Socrates, you may be sure, did not join in these sarcasms. Sparta had shown the honour and manhood that history can teach, and how it can make of men champions of their country, keepers of their forefathers' fame, and rivals of their own ancient heroes.

Side by side with this ancient instance we may put one of our own day. There is a country which has suddenly risen to great eminence in war and organisation, as it had long been famous in the arts, with which England hastened to make alliance. That country is Japan. In Japan, when the eldest son comes of age, it is the custom for his father to take him a tour on foot round the country, visiting every place of fame in its history, so that the youth may enter on man's estate as a worthy citizen of the State that bred him. These honourable pilgrims can be met on every road. They have known, like the men of Sparta, the power of history to fortify the mind and expand the soul. Every Japanese man of character will tell you that in any serious enterprise he is in the presence, in the company of the great Dead of his people. That by them his purpose is ennobled, his courage uplifted, his solitude changed into a great communion. We have seen how that spirit has exalted a people.

With such instances in our minds we may ask what we are doing in Ireland. What kind of citizens are we building up for our own land?

As in England, so in Ireland, history has in the last dozen years been made compulsory in the schools. But there is a difference. For Ireland history is not a subject in itself. In our primary and intermediate education Irish history is now a department of English language and literature. At the age when impressions made on a youth's mind are certain to become the all-compelling habits of his later life, it is suggested to him that the history of his country is less important than the rules of English grammar, and that the achievements of his father may at the best rank with the model sentences in which English essayists write of Friendship and Gardens and Christmas. The student for honours under the Intermediate system may, at his own will, prefer a continental language to history. A pass-student might choose to gain all the necessary marks in English grammar and composition alone; if he has drunk in all that the amiable and unimportant Alexander Smith can tell him "Of the Importance of a Man to Himself," he may omit all that the world can tell him "Of the Importance of a Man to his Country," or of his Country to him. Such knowledge may be left to the "idiots and foolish people, who only amuse themselves to know the succession of kings, and establishing and declination of estates, and such-like trash of flim-flam tales."

Nor is this the worst of the matter. Suppose that an Irish boy has been stirred by what he has seen in his country home. There was, perhaps, beside it a Danes' Fort, a Giants' Ring, one of the two thousand mounds piled up in Ireland by human hands, a Rathcroghan, or a mighty Ailech of the kings where legendary monarchs sleep on their horses waiting for the day that shall call them to ride out. He may have lived by a solemn burial place of great chiefs, by a round tower, by a high cross deeply carved, by some island of saints rich in ruins and sculptured slabs. He may have been taken to the Irish Academy and seen the Psalter of Columcille; or to Trinity College to look on the book of Kells; or to the National Museum to be turned loose among the carved rocks, the copper cauldrons, the golden diadems and torques, the mighty horns of bronze, the heavy Danish swords, the weights for commerce, the marvels in metal and enamel work, the Tara brooch, the Ardagh chalice, the Cross of Cong, the long array of crosiers and bells and shrines and book-covers. He may learn by chance that his country is the wonder of Europe for the wealth and beauty of its relics of the past. Desire may come on him to know the story of a land so astonishing in the visible records left by his ancestors. Descended from a race who had history in their very blood and the glorious tradition of their fathers, he may feel that old hereditary passion burn in his heart. He will add history to his study of the English language and the essays of Smith.

But even in that case, once entered on the course of education provided for him by the Intermediate Board, he will find through the whole of his pass work or of his honour work not one word to tell him who made the marvels he has seen. For in Anglicised Ireland it is ordered that history shall begin in 1066. The Irish annals record a comet in that year. But it is not for the comet the year is chosen, but because the date of the Norman Conquest of England is to mark the beginning of history for Ireland.

From the first the student is caught by the pleasant fiction which is now proclaimed on every Unionist platform that Ireland "under the English ownership," has no life save that which England gives. Irish history is not to be the story of Ireland, but of the "United Kingdom." It is to travel with the fortunes of England step by step. An exact care conducts the student through the centuries. All dates are ruled by English text-books, never by periods of change in Ireland. According to the step by step theory, if the Irish student must begin his story of Ireland with William's Conquest of England, he must pause at the end of the English Wars of the Roses. What matter if that close of a period in England happens in Ireland to be in full midway of a very extraordinary racial and constitutional movement full of vital energy? The teacher must by order cut his story in half, and start again to pull up his next course sharply at the death of Elizabeth, a merely nominal date in Ireland, which ended or began nothing. There the next period opens by order, and ended this present year at a date (1784) when it would be absolutely impossible for an Irish teacher to call a halt except by stopping in the middle of a sentence; and for the coming year is to close at 1760, before the first movement for the emancipation of the Irish Parliament. Not a word will the Irish youth hear of the Irish kingdoms and schools and craftsmen and merchants, nor of the Danes and their fleets, nor of the Irish culture spread over Europe. He would know nothing of Columcille and the work of Iona, nor of Columbanus and the work of St. Gall and of Bobio. Nothing will be told of St. Brendan and his sailing to the west; nor of learned Fergil the Geometer, who in spite of the orthodox theories of an impassable equator, alone maintained that there were living men at the antipodes; nor of the Irish goldsmiths and builders. Cormac's chapel must go. The very name of Brian Boru is expunged. There can be no mention of the five hundred years of Irishmen's fame in Europe as classical scholars, philosophers, saints, merchants, or travellers. The centuries of Ireland's history as a free and independent country are blotted out, and he may catch no glimpse of his people save in the various phases of their material subjugation. During his entire course he can turn no wandering eye on an Ireland that had any art, literature, or industry of its own—a place where anything may have happened on its own account, or where any interest may lie detached from an English book of chronology.

This disastrous conception of the "Union" as a kind of amalgamation of countries in which all national limits are submerged and lost follows the Irishman at home and abroad. He can scarcely set foot in Europe save in the track of Irish wanderers of every age whose fame should be his glory. But the shadow of this distorted notion hangs round him—the shadow of the predominant sharer of all the effort and fortune of his people. In the published Catalogue of the MSS. in the Royal Library at Brussels, he must look for the Irish Annals and historical documents under the one heading *Angleterre*, without even a sub-heading *Irlande*. In Switzerland, surrounded by relics of the six hundred and thirteen dependent houses of St. Gall, whence Irish monks restored civilization to that land, he will be told at S. Beatenberg by the guide-books that S. Beatus was *British*, and by local tradition that he was Scotch. At the shrine of San Pellegrino in the Apennines, he will hear praises of a *Scotch* king's son. In Rome he will learn that *England* was "the Isle of Saints." Against these ignorances his training in Ireland gives him no protection. Similar fallacies pursue him across the Atlantic. Let him go to America, and Washington Irving will tell him of the mariner whose story was one of the moving causes that led Columbus to enquire of the land beyond the Ocean, and will inform him that this famous St. Brendan was a *Scotch*monk. Many others he will find ignorant of history, and above all anxious not to identify Ireland with any of her children that have done great things. Mr. Whitelaw Reid will explain to him that the emigrants from Ulster to America, the Ulster-born leaders who fought for American independence in counsel, in convention, and in the field; the "Sons of St. Patrick" who poured out their money and their blood for Washington—that all these were *Scotchmen*, of no Irish kin or race, whose followers and descendants have manfully rejected the term "Scotch-Irish" because it "confused the race with the accident of birth," and called themselves "Ulster Scots" to show they had no part or lot with the Irish by blood (*Celtic Review*, Jan., 1912). He apparently sees in the Presbyterian religion of the "Ulster Scot" some subtle evidence of a nobler and more distinguished origin than the "Scotch Irish," some guarantee of Low-German or English stock.

The new school of American Irish, who under the influence of the "Anglo-Saxon" enthusiasm, or with a desire to be on the winning side, lay claim to a "Scotch" descent, ignore the historical meaning of the word "Scot," or the origin of the name "Scotland." In vain for them authentic history may tell of the ceaseless wanderings of the Gaelic people across the narrow seas. From Ireland the Scots in early times spread over the Hebrides and western Highlands, and carried their settlements and speech over the Lowlands of the Picts and Britons to the very borders of the little English colony of the Lothians, leaving the western and middle Lowlands the most Celtic region in Scotland. Irish folk settled freely in Scotland until the confiscation of Ulster; as for example when the Monroes and Currys crossed the sea, about 1300, with a number of other noble families who obtained grants of land. Intermarriage was very frequent at all times. Back to Ireland again came streams of immigrants from the "Scot" or Irish settlements across the water. The mingled race of Celts and Norse from the Hebrides and the Highlands, all alike talking Irish and claiming Irish descent, poured colonies into Ireland without ceasing from 1250 to 1600, forefathers of hundreds of thousands to-day of Irish family. The western and middle Lowlands (along with the Highlands) sent from 1600 the main body of settlers of the Ulster Plantation, chiefly of Picto-Celtic stock; most of the first settlers must have been bi-lingual, speaking not only "Broad Scots" but their native Gaelic, which in 1589 was still the chief language of Galloway. Scots and Irish were the same to Henry VIII., whose servant Alen protested in 1549 against any "liberty" for the Irish, which, he said, was "the only thing that Scots and wild Irish constantly contended for." The Scots of the Isles were known to Elizabeth as "those Yrishe people," "the Yrishes"; the "English Scots" whom she employed in her Irish wars were so called from their political faction and Protestant religion, not from any difference of blood from their brethren. In 1630 the scholar Bedell included Irish and Scots in one single group; "and surely it was a work agreeable to the mind of God that the poor Irish, being a very numerous nation, besides the greater half of Scotland, and all those islands called Hebrides, that lie in the Irish Sea, and many of the Orcades also that speak Irish, should be enabled to search the Scriptures." The old Irish of Ulster in 1641 excepted the Scots from their hostile measures as being of their own race, and this only a generation after the Plantation, when most of the evicted Irish must have been still alive. Jeremy Taylor in 1667 describes the Scots and Irish of north-east Ulster as "*populus unius labii* and unmingled with others." Over whole districts, where half the population at least were Presbyterian descendants of Scottish immigrants, the speech of the people even in the eighteenth century was Gaelic. For some fourteen centuries indeed common schools of learning, a common literature, common national festivals, maintained the unbroken tradition of unity of race; it was from Ireland, in an Irish translation, that the Bible reached the Highlands. The kings of Scotland long kept the remembrance of their connexion with the remote generations of the race of Gaedhel Glas. Dr. Norman Moore in his "Medicine in the British Isles," (149) has preserved a Highland tradition told him by Field-Marshal Sir Patrick Grant whose memory was full of the old Gaelic stories and verses; that at the Scottish coronation of Charles I. ancient Gaelic phrases of installation were used for the last time.

Among the men whom Mr. Whitelaw Reid selects to give glory to the "Scotch" race as distinguished from the Irish, we may take at chance three examples. President MacKinlay came of the Hebridean race of Gaelic Scots with a strong infusion of Norse blood, who, Norsemen and Scots alike, boasted of Irish descent; they settled in Ireland about 1400 A.D., nor did the Antrim MacKinlays in later days ever speak of themselves save as Irish. President Monroe belonged to an Irish Gaelic family which had crossed to Scotland with a number of other noble families about 1300, and obtained grants of land among their kin there. Patrick Henry, whether he was of old Ulster race or of the Scottish lowlands, unless clear proof to the contrary can be given by a detailed pedigree, must be counted as a Celt or a Picto-Celt: one group of Henrys in Ulster is descended from the MacHenry sept of the O'Neills who lived on the Bann-side at the time of the Plantation; another family, more ancient and probably more numerous, O h-Inneirghe, whose surname is now written Henry, was the ruling sept of a district in the south of Derry country. No one, unless he proves his case by direct evidence, could truthfully and with knowledge assert that Patrick Henry, or President Monroe, or President MacKinlay, were other than representative Celts by race.

It would have been a strange doctrine to the Irish emigrants themselves to tell them that they were Scotch. From 1720 they swarmed over to people Pennsylvania, as if, men said at the time, Ireland was sending out all its inhabitants—in one year alone (1729) no less than 5,655 Irish, to 267 English and Welsh, and 43 Scotch. There was a Scotch Society of St. Andrew's in Philadelphia (1749); but the emigrants from Ireland, Catholic and Presbyterian alike, looked on themselves as plain Irishmen, not Scotch; they gave to their settlements Irish names; the wealthier men among them established in 1765 an "Irish Club"; out of this they formed in 1771 the leading Irish organisation before and during the Revolution —the famous Society of the "Friendly Sons of St. Patrick." There were at first but three Catholics in the Society, but the Irish Presbyterians and Episcopalians of that day chose for their patron the Saint of Ireland, not of Scotland, and for their President a Catholic, Moylan, certainly not a Scotchman; they met on St. Patrick's Day; their medal bore figures of *Hibernia* with a harp, and *St. Patrick* carrying a cross and trampling on a snake. The heroic services of that devoted Society of Irishmen cannot be told here. After the war it founded and became merged in the *Hibernian* Society of "the natives of Ireland or descendants of Irishmen" (so little did they fear the name), for the relief of emigrants from Ireland. These Irishmen had not yet learned to despise their race and country, and to invent for themselves a new nation without any root in history.

In English history, where certain general lines of knowledge have been laid down as the common property of educated men, serious lapses are held a reproach: in Irish history an ambassador from the United States to Great Britain and Ireland can allow himself to tell us that an "Ulster Scot" is no more an Irishman than a man would be a horse if born in a stable.

The imaginations of a mock "Imperial history," by which all treasure found is thrown "impartially" into the common stock of the United Kingdom, in other words of Great Britain, leaving Ireland bare, belong not to science but to politics. By such a perverted history the honourable pride of a people may be transformed into humiliation and self-distrust. They are made to stand before Europe with the appearance of defeat, ruin, and rebuke; a race without the dignity of ever having had a true civilization, incapable of development in the land they wasted. What vigour or self-respect can grow out of a maimed history such as this? Or can any promise of material advancement serve as the substitute for a good reputation, or consolation for spiritual impoverishment?

We may take one notable instance of how since the Union ignorance of Irish history has been officially fostered. In 1828 a lofty enterprise was opened by Sir Thomas Larcom, director of the central office of the newly-appointed Irish Ordnance Survey. The Survey maps were to be constructed on such a scale as to be of use in correcting the unequal pressure of taxation, and to serve as guides for local improvement. Enquiry indeed was needed into the resources and conditions of a country which Petrie describes—"the habitations of the people miserable and comfortless, and the people themselves the most wretched in the world. Joy will never brighten the prospect, misery never disappear." To carry out these orders Larcom planned a scheme on noble lines. He held it necessary to complete the maps by making a study in each parish of the state in which Nature had placed it, the condition to which it had been brought by art, and the uses now made by the people of their combination; in other words, there must be an exact knowledge of the natural products of the country, its history and antiquities, and its economic state and social condition. In this scheme of elevated science an enquiry into past history was considered necessary as a prelude to the proper understanding of the present state—an enquiry which was to include all monuments of the past, Pagan and Christian, all the traditions and accounts of them that remained, the state of society in which they arose, the earliest history of the people whose descendants might still inhabit the district, and the changes which led to the present establishments for government.

The opportunity for carrying out this work was as surprising as its conception. The great scholar Petrie, who was at the time founding the museum of the Royal Irish Academy and in great measure founding too its library, was in 1833 set at the head of the historical department of the Survey, and charged with the task of collecting the true names of baronies, townlands, and parishes, and the investigation of ancient monuments. He gathered round him a staff of Irish scholars—men of the soil, heirs of the Irish tradition—John O'Donovan, Eugene O'Curry, J. O'Connor, P. O'Keefe, along with Clarence Mangan, Du Noyer, Wakeman, and others, all filled with the same spirit, and fired with the desire of producing a perfect work. Never perhaps had there been such a combination of talent directed to the one end of restoring Irish knowledge. For the first time during centuries of exclusion, Irish students were brought into close and constant communication in their own country with men of trained intelligence, and encouraged to use their skill for the benefit of their country. Once more Ireland had such a school as those which in the periods of her great revivals in the twelfth and fifteenth centuries gathered up and left to us all the relics of Irish history that we possess. Once more a kind of peripatetic University was set up, in the very spirit of the older Irish life.

The astonishing enthusiasm of these zealots is shown by the almost incredible record of their work in half a dozen years. It is such things as these that reveal to us the soul of Irish Nationality and the might of its repression. We can but stand astonished before the unstinted labour, before the miraculous accomplishment, of that company of workers. The work was new, travel was slow, and hardship frequent: but every difficulty vanished before their consuming ardour. Petrie's band has left, besides maps, sketches, and documents of a general nature, not less than four hundred and sixty-eight large volumes of documents relating to Irish topography, language, history, and antiquities. A collection was made of over sixty thousand names, of their mutations, their various spellings, their meanings, and translations in English; when this work was completed a skilled Irish scholar was sent to every district to learn there from Irish speakers the vernacular name, and to collect traditions and legends, and note any antiquities that had been omitted. The traditions of Ireland at that time had not been wholly broken. In Petrie's writings we can still see the Irish multitudes who in the depth of their poverty preserved the memories of their race and their holy places, and the national pilgrims gathering round their old shrines "with the utmost fervency of devotion, and in all their movements an abstracted intensity of feeling that carries the mind back to remote times." In spite of much destruction, in spite of the lamentable absence in the new landlords of

Ireland of proper pride and national feeling, there still remained a mass of ancient monuments preserved by the pious memories of the people, crosses, graveyards, old paths, and names and histories; which have been since swept away in the horrors of famine and emigration and the devastating land commercialism let loose by the Encumbered Estates Act.

The first memoir published by the Ordnance Survey in 1837, the account of Derry, was hailed with universal enthusiasm. "Irishmen of all sects and parties felt that in such work as this they would have for the first time the materials for a true history of their country." But the Government interfered. The Topographical Survey was closed, the staff discharged, and the vast mass of material, comprising among other things upwards of four hundred quarto volumes of letters and documents relating to the topography, language, history, antiquities, productions, and social state of almost every county in Ireland, were ordered to be kept, idle and useless, in the Survey Office at Mountjoy barracks. The reason given was the cost. At this time England was drawing from Ireland to her own use some three millions a year above her expenditure there. It was shown that the sale of the memoir was such as would probably defray the whole expense. The Government objected to treating history and political economy as subjects which might re-open questions of Irish party divisions: it was answered that the events of history could not be buried in oblivion, since they had occurred and their effects continue, and it was well for the public to have a plain impartial record of bare facts, since on neither side were the facts yet known.

In answer to the vehement protests of all Ireland, a Commission was appointed under a new Government in 1843. It advised that the work should be continued, and urged the importance of the time, for monuments and language were alike disappearing: it recommended that the vast mass of collected material now lying waste should be published, since "no enquirer until the officers of the Survey commenced their labours, has ever brought an equal amount of local knowledge, sound criticism, and accurate acquaintance with the Irish language to bear upon it." The Government took no notice. It was believed by the best-informed that some strong concealed influence urged on ministers that it was dangerous to open up to the people the memory of their fathers and their old society, or remind them of the boundaries of their clans and families. In vain the best Irishmen of the day, of every race and religion, pleaded for a braver view of truth and statesmanship. Political influences, the fears of absentee landlords or of a Protestant ascendancy, prevailed in London. English rulers dreaded the knowledge of the Irish more than they dreaded their ignorance; and the door was shut on history, science, and truth, with the results that we have seen in succeeding generations.

By this act much knowledge was finally obliterated: no such opportunity can ever occur again. Much more was set back for a hundred years, and ignorance still left enthroned. We may still hear men professing, as though time had stood still, the doctrines Petrie reported in vogue a century ago: "The history and antiquities of Ireland previous to the English Invasion, are wholly unworthy of notice, or, at best, involved in obscurity and darkness such as no sane mind would venture to penetrate." Irish history, buried by two Governments, was supposed to have no resurrection: instead of the serious enquiry inaugurated by the old Survey, modern statesmen will assure us through Mr. Balfour that for talk of Irish ideas and institutions, "there is no historic basis whatever."

The Royal Irish Academy applied for the custody of a part of the Survey records, which were given to its keeping in 1860; and have there been consulted for local or county histories. Meanwhile the Survey was continued in an innocuous form without the historic virus. Directed from Southampton, English "division officers" in Dublin, Belfast and Cork conduct the Irish Survey. Their maps may serve practical purposes of buying and selling land, and even present accurately all modern features, police barracks and the like. But they offer doubtful help to the curious historian on the road of scientific enquiry. The spirit and purpose of the older research has been banished. Irish antiquities are no longer objects of interest or of skilled observation; Irish names are treated in many cases as an insurmountable difficulty; any ordered attempt at their right spelling is abandoned. The ancient fort of Lisnalinchy in Antrim has been allotted the happy name of *Silentia*, as if to give to a deep-buried Irish history the respectability of a mock Roman tombstone. Port-na-veadog, the port of the plover, appears as Dog's Bay. Professor

Macalister, examining the ancient ruins on the Carrowkeel mountain in Co. Sligo, has reported there the remarkable site of one of the oldest village settlements in northern Europe, with remains of over forty-seven structures; and hard by an ancient cemetery with fourteen carns left by the old builders. The Survey has been there, and has marked the height of the beacon it erected on one of the finest of the carns, but has left on the map no record of this conspicuous and striking carn as an ancient monument. The most important of the structures, eighty-seven feet in diameter and twenty-five in height, is marked by an indefinite symbol, and not as having anycharacter of antiquity. While nearly all the chief carns were omitted, by some chance or curious scruple of conscience one or two of the smaller examples have been noted. Of twenty-three place names in the square mile of country only nine are recorded. Names here and elsewhere are set down in an Anglicised and phonetic spelling, often atrocious in form. As Professor Macalister observes, nothing could more clearly prove than this characteristic effort of the Ordnance Survey in Ireland the absolute necessity of a thorough re-survey, under expert superintendence, of the archæology and place names of the country. All historians, all Irishmen alike, must ardently join in such an entreaty, for the honour of their land. Is it too much to hope that this national work may not be for ever left to indifferent hands, but that Irish scholars may yet be given the patriotic task of saving what yet remains on Irish soil of the inheritance of her people.

Of one thing, however, we may be sure. The reform of Irish history must begin in our own country, among our own people. Since it is public opinion that at the last decides what our people shall learn of their fatherland, we ourselves must be the keepers of our fame and the makers of our history. Let us in Ireland therefore remember that we have an ancestry on which there is no need for us to cry shame. Chivalry, learning, patriotism, poetry, have been found there, even "in huts to which an Englishman would have hesitated to give the name of a house." No people have ever surpassed them in exaltation or intensity of spiritual life. The sun has risen and set in that land on lives of courage, honour, and beauty. The seasons have watched the undying effort to make Ireland the honoured home of a united people. Not a field that has not drunk in the blood of men and women poured out for the homes of their fathers.

Why should not we, the sons and daughters of Ireland, take our rich inheritance? "Let us enjoy, whenever we have an opportunity, the delight of admiration, and perform the duties of reverence." So long as the Spirit of life is over us, I do not know, and I hope you do not know, why we in this country should not be worthy of our dead.

CHAPTER II

THE TRADE ROUTES OF IRELAND.

A DISCUSSION of the Trade Routes of Ireland may seem to some a superfluous and barren task. It has long been a fashion to look on the country as an island, "remote, unfriended, melancholy, slow." Writers have pictured it as lying through the centuries in primitive barbarism, an outlying desolation of poverty and disorder. The blame of this desolation is sometimes laid on the savagery of the people, sometimes on the position of the island, at the very "ends of the earth." No doubt there has been a certain political convenience in the very usual argument that the geographical position of Ireland, lying so near to Great Britain, makes it immediately dependent on that country alone, so that it could by nature have no real converse with Europe, and no door of civilisation save through England. An island beyond an island—such is reputed the forlorn position of Ireland. We all naturally believe that which we constantly hear or frequently repeat: and it is well from time to time to ask ourselves what reason may lie behind common tradition—in this special case to enquire what geography and history may have to tell us of the natural trade routes of Ireland and of England in former times.

From the map it is plain that the two islands have a very different outlook. Michelet has pictured Europe with all her main rivers and harbours opening to the west, and the island of Great Britain alone lying as a mighty ship poised on the ocean with her prow fronting the orient.

The Thames opens its harbour to the east, the capital looks to the east, and the early trading centres, the Cinque Ports, turn to the sunrising. Thus the natural way of trade and travel from England to the Continent has always been by the narrow seas—across the Channel or the North Sea to the convenient river-mouths and harbours of the north European plain. Ireland was in a different case. If the opposite British coast, for the most part inhospitable mountain and forest, offered to her in early times a slender trade and a harsh welcome, she on her side did not turn to it her best natural ports. Those on the east coast from Waterford to Belfast are few; Dublin, left to itself, is a poor harbour; and from thence to Belfast there is only one small port, Ardglass, where the entrance is safe at low tide. The chief harbours of Ireland in fact were those that swelled with the waves of the Atlantic Ocean. Her outlook was across its stormy waters, and her earliest traffic through the perils of the Gaulish sea. The English were concerned with the north and east of Europe, the Irish with the south and west, and their paths did not cross.

For Ireland, therefore, the road to Europe did not lie across Great Britain. As far back as we can see into the primitive darkness the inhabitants of the island were all in turn out on the great seas. An old myth or legend tells of the ancient Manannan Mac Lir, "Son of the Sea," who was the best pilot that was in the west of Europe, and the greatest reader of the sky and weather: or who in another tale appears a sea-god triumphant over the ocean as his boat raced under him on the immensity of the waters like a chariot on the summer fields, while he sang in his joy —"That is to me a happy plain with a profusion of flowers, looking from the chariot of two wheels." Ireland, in times beyond the reach of history, lay on the high-road of an ancient trade between the countries we know as Scandinavia and Gaul. Even in the Stone age its people cut some of their flint arrows after the fashion of Portugal, or carried them from that peninsula across the Bay of Biscay; and fragments of stone cups have been found in Ireland, as in Britain, which are said to have come from the Mediterranean by the Gaulish sea. As for the northern traffic, we have traces of it more than a thousand years before the Christian era in burial mounds of the Bronze age, where there are stones carved with a form of ornament which in western Europe is only found in Scandinavia and Ireland.

It was during the Bronze age that the first Gaelic or Goidelic invaders entered Ireland, coming not through Britain but over-sea from Spain and Gaul, from the openings of the Garonne and the Loire, or from the ports of Brittany. And by that open highway sailed also later settlers from southern and northern Gaul. Some relics of these conquering tribes, fine rivetted trumpets of bronze made after the fashion of the continent, of the same pattern as those used in central France about the Loire, show that they kept up intercourse with their people abroad. For centuries, in fact, this intercourse can be traced. An invasion of the Gauls in the third century B.C. left to Leinster its old name of Laigen, from the broad-headed lances which they carried; and five hundred years later, in the second century A.D., Irish princes used to send to Gaul for soldiers to serve in their wars.

In the time of the Roman Empire therefore Irish trade with Europe was already well established. Tacitus (A.D. 98) tells that its ports and harbours were well known to merchants; and in the second century the geographer Ptolemy of Alexandria gave a list, very surprising for the time, of the river-mouths, mountains, and port towns of Ireland, and its sea-coast tribes—a knowledge he may have gained from Marinus of Tyre, or the Syrian traders who conducted the traffic from Asia Minor to the Rhone, and thence across the Gaulish Sea. Italy exported her wine in the second century B.C.; and in the second century A.D., four hundred years later, when wine was grown on the hill sides of Provence it may have reached Irish ports, transported by merchants of Marseilles to the Garonne, or by the valleys of the Rhone and the Loire, and thence across the sea. They travelled in ships built to confront Atlantic gales, with high poops standing out of the water like castles, and great leathern sails—stout hulls that were steered and worked by the born sailors of the Breton coast. From Brittany the passage to Ireland could be made in three days. From the Loire it was two days longer, as we may see from a later Irish story of the sixth century which tells how a ship-load of strangers, five decades of them, came sailing from the lands of Latium on pilgrimage to Ireland. Each decade of pilgrims took with them an Irish saint to guide and protect the vessel, every one in his turn for a day and a night, which gives a voyage of five days and nights. As they neared the Irish coast a fierce storm arose, and St. Senan, who was that day guardian of the company, rose from dinner with a thigh-bone in his hand, and blessing the air with the bone brought the pilgrims safe into Cork harbour. The saint was a practical sailor and pilot, and he had been allotted the best joint, the portion which by Irish law was given to the king or the high poet.

But while traders of the Empire sailed to Ireland, the armies of Rome never crossed the Irish Sea. Ireland therefore lay outside the Roman Empire, while it lay within the circle of imperial civilisation and commerce. Christianity first came from across the Gaulish Sea, and the art of writing, and new forms of ornament. From Gaul the Irish learned to divide tribe-land into private property marked by boundary stones. Roman-Hellenistic learning, which spread from northern Italy to Marseilles, crossed the Irish seas with the merchants of Aquitaine carrying the wine of Bordeaux; or it was brought home by Irish scholars of the fourth century who went to seek learning in Narbonne, where Greek was spoken as a living tongue. The Irish Pelagius, who went to Italy in 400, was able to carry on a discussion in Jerusalem in 415 with Orosius the Spaniard, in which he spoke Greek while Orosius needed an interpreter: if he had not learned Greek in Ireland, Zimmer reminds us, he would not have been able to learn it in Rome. Nearly two hundred years later, in 595, the Irish saint Columbanus and his companions knew Greek, but Gregory the Great did not know it, though he had twice been Papal nuncio in Constantinople. Ovid and Vergil were known and read in Ireland, where scholars seem to have taken all that Rome had to give of classical culture and philosophy.

It is often assumed that to share in the benefits of an empire it is necessary to be a subject country, lying within its police control, and that the Irish suffered by never having been forced under the authority of Rome. Perhaps, however, we might learn here another lesson—that in matters of civilisation what is really needed is not subjection to force, but free human converse and the willing intercourse of men. We have the spectacle of an island beyond the military rule, the police control, the law, of the Roman empire, willingly adopting all the spiritual good which Rome could give it, and the culture that the intelligence of its people found to suit them. Free to keep her own customs, Ireland could gain this new learning without losing her own civilization and her pride of language, history, and law. It was in seas of blood that such national pride was wiped out by Roman conquerors from the plains of Gaul. But for the Irish at that time there was no violent breach with the traditions of their race, nor any humiliation or bondage to darken their high spirit; and in the joyful and brilliant activity of the succeeding centuries they illustrated the free and peaceful union of two civilizations.

Ireland had another advantage from her place of freedom on the open highways of the sea. For lying outside the Empire she was saved from the economic ruin that fell on all the Roman dominions when, by the fatal policy of the Empire, enterprise and wealth were sucked to the centre and capital, draining the provinces bare; so that, for example, witnesses of that time describe the once wealthy port of Cadiz as a town of great empty warehouses, silent and deserted, save for a few poor old men and women creeping about its melancholy streets. Her position saved her too when the barbarians swept over the Empire. As she had been unconquered by the Romans so she remained unconquered by Teuton or English. Her learning did not perish before invaders; and if on the mainland every old line of communication was closed or broken, her way of the ocean was still free. It is true that the wars of the English invaders of Britain for some hundred and fifty years (449-597) barred all passage through it to the Continent. But that route had never been of any real consequence. A way to Europe across Britain was no doubt known to the Irish in Roman times, and some pilgrims journeyed by that way across the Empire. But this was not the main route for travellers from Ireland, and it was never the line of their continental trade. There seems to have been little communication on the whole with Britain. Settlers went over from Ireland to Scotland, to Wales, to the Cornish peninsula, and founded Irish colonies. But in the main the Irish troubled themselves very little about Britain at all. In fact from the third century onwards they were accustomed to give to all strangers the name of "Galls," from Gallos, the people of Gaul, the chief visitors they knew.

To the Irish the important thing therefore was that the way of the sea was still open. Traders from Gaul sailed along the western coast, and up the Shannon to Roscommon and Loch Cé, and on the eastern side their ships passed by the Irish Sea to what is now Down and Antrim, to Iona, and Cantyre. They still as of old carried the wine of Provence in great wooden tuns, in one of which three men could stand upright; there still came men speaking Greek, and scholars of the east, and artists of Gaul. At this time indeed the Irish were no recluse people, living in a backwater or severed from the great world. An Old Irish poem tells of the traditions of Leinster under its ancient kings—"The sweet strain heard there at every hour; its wine-barque upon the purple flood; its shower of silver of great splendour; its torques of gold from the lands of the Gaul." The metropolis of Columcille's church organization at Iona, the established centre of Irish learning at Bangor in Down, both alike lay in the track of the sailing ships, and in frequent communication with Europe. News of the destruction by earthquake of Citta Nuova in Istria was brought to Columcille that same year by Gaulish mariners. Columbanus and his companions could take ship from Bangor to Nantes on their mission to Europe (589). Northwards Irishmen sailed to the Hebrides, the Orkneys, the Shetlands. They seem to have traded and married with Scandinavians a century before the invasion of Ireland by the Wikings. Moreover Irishmen had travelled as far as Iceland in 795, where Nadoddr the Norseman heard of them some sixty years later.

Thus the old civilization, rudely interrupted elsewhere, was carried on unbroken in Ireland. Now was the time (500-1000) when the island began to give back to Europe the treasures of learning which she had stored up in the time of the Roman Empire, and had kept safely through the barbarian wars. Missionaries and scholars from Iona and Ireland carried letters and Christian teaching to every part of England, while ship-loads of Englishmen went to Ireland for instruction. Other Irishmen sailed to Brittany, and journeyed east over northern France beyond the Rhine. A greater number travelled by Nantes, Angers, Tours, past the monastery of Columbanus at Lisieux, and thence over middle Europe, or by St. Gall southward through Italy as far as Tarentum, and to the Holy Land. Occasionally pilgrims and missionaries took the road to Europe through Britain, when with the settlement of the English kingdoms and the coming of Augustine (597) a new intercourse had opened between the English and the continental peoples. That is, some few travellers went this way, but merchants still kept to the old sea route, and the greater number of Irish pilgrims and scholars. It was by that way, for example, according to the old story by a monk of St. Gall, that two Scots from Ireland sailed to Gaul in the early days of Charles the Great, and in the market-place, where the merchants trafficked with the crowds, raised their cry of an Irish trade:—"If anyone is desirous of wisdom, let him come to us and receive it, for we have it to sell." At last they were brought to Charles himself, who asked what payment they would need; nothing more, they answered, than convenient situations, ingenious minds, and as living in a foreign country to be supplied with food and raiment; and the king formed a school for one of them in France, and set the other at the head of the great school at Pavia. Irish monasteries, one after another in rapid order, rose along the main highways of travel, among the ruined heaps of Roman towns where wild beasts alone found shelter, in forest and desert and mountain. Every school had Irish teachers and Irish manuscripts, relics of which still remain in continental libraries. Ireland became the source of culture to all Germanic nations: indeed wherever in the seventh and following centuries education or knowledge is found it may be traced directly or indirectly to Irish influence. It has been justly said that at the time of Charles the Bald every one who spoke Greek on the Continent was almost certainly an Irishman, or taught by an Irishman. By degrees Irish monasteries, built and supported by Irish money, spread over Europe from Holland to Tarentum, from Gaul to Bulgaria.

The Continent was therefore well known to Ireland when about 800 A.D. a new revolution passed over Europe.

Continental trade, as we have seen, had perished with the Roman Empire. Commerce had fallen to its lowest point. There was scarcely any money, nor in any country, neither England, nor France, nor Germany, a native class of merchants; wandering Jews and Greeks and Syrians, and later Italians, carried on what little buying and selling still survived. On the shores of the North Sea, however, the Frisians had made their town of Duurstede, near the mouth of the Rhine, a centre for traffic carried down the river; and in their stout, flat-bottomed, high-boarded sailing ships traded across the North Sea and the Baltic. Duurstede became for a time the chief port of western Europe. There Charles the Great coined money, and the lines along which the Frisian traders carried their wares may still be traced by the finding of the Duurstede coins. But even in the time of the Emperor Charles came the change which was to sweep away the Frisian traders. This was the rise of the new lords of the sea—the Scandinavians—who were to wrest commerce from Frisians and Gauls, and open a new trade for northern Europe.

The Scandinavians got their training in a hard school. They had a thousand miles of stormy shores to practice seamanship, fishing along their mountain coasts, and sailing against Arctic tempests round the North Cape. They had to build better ships than anyone else, and to sail them better. They invented a new kind of vessel where both oars and sails were used. And in a short time the Frisians were outdone both in seamanship and in trade.

East and west the Scandinavians sailed. As early as the eight century colonies of Swedes were passing by the Baltic and the gulf of Finland to settle on the opposite coast about Novgorod and along the Dnieper—the East way, as they called it. They left Scandinavian names along the rapids of the river as their travellers pushed forward, till in 839 they came in contact with the Greeks, and Swedes who had journeyed by the Dnieper were introduced by the Emperor of the East to the Western Emperor Louis the Pious. Their ships were soon the terror of the Black Sea shores—laden with warriors tall like palm trees, ruddy, fairhaired, who were in turn traders and plunderers, conquerors and slave-dealers. In 865 two hundred of their vessels appeared before Constantinople; in 880 they had reached the Sea of Azof, the Don and the Volga; in 913 they had five hundred ships, each carrying a hundred men, in the Caspian. Novgorod was the mart of their vast eastern commerce. There have been found in Sweden nearly twenty thousand Arabian coins, dating from 698 to 1002 A.D., carried across the Baltic by home-going merchants. Gothland became the general centre of exchange for the Eastway trade, where Danes sailed from their settlements on the Mecklenburg coast and the mouth of the Oder, to buy Russian furs, Greek and Arabian silks, and Indian spices, and here have been discovered thirteen thousand coins of the tenth and eleventh centuries—Byzantine, Arabian, and from central Asia.

Other adventurers from Norway and Denmark turned towards the Atlantic Ocean, trading and plundering in every harbour of the west, as far as Seville and the Spanish coasts. Northward they peopled Iceland and the Orkneys, and in time rounded the North Cape. They fished the Ocean for whales, and opened a trade in whale-meat and in the furs and cod of the White Sea with Normandy and England. The English liked better to buy than to catch whales. "Can you take a whale?" we read in an old West-Saxon dialogue. "Many," says the home-loving Englishman, "take whales without danger, and then they get a great price, but I dare not from the fearfulness of my mind."

Besides opening out this world-wide trade, the Scandinavians made a revolution also in the manner of trading. Up to this time buying and selling had been carried on by travelling dealers, Syrian and Italian. Now however Norsemen and Danes, who had no towns in their own lands, planted themselves in their new countries in fortified cities; and, for example, showed their enterprise by forming in the Five Danish Burghs in England the earliest federation of towns known outside Italy. In the new towns a settled class of merchants was established, who learned to group themselves according to the English system of guilds. The Scandinavians learned also to strike coins after the manner of the Frisians. In all these ways, by their new ships, their new trade routes, their money, their guilds, and their settled merchants in towns, the Scandinavians won a pre-eminence on the sea, which they were to hold in their own hands for some two hundred years.

What was the effect in Ireland of this new peril, an attack on Europe from the sea? In the first place the highways of the sea, never before closed, were barred by the Scandinavian free-booters. A few Irish travellers (even from Leinster) did even in 800 and 850 take the old accustomed journey to the Loire and so across France to Germany; but the passage was now dangerous. The terrors of the sea journey drove travellers to the land route, and the way across England to the Continent became so important that clerics of the tenth century could not imagine that any other way had ever been possible. The new sea-kings, moreover, were not the people to forget the ancient and profitable trade routes of the wine commerce, or the Irish harbours into which trading ships from north and south had sailed for the last two thousand years, or the gold that had been dug from Irish mines in old days. They seized every harbour, sent their boats up every creek and river, plundered the monasteries and wealthy houses, broke into every burial mound for treasure, and put a poll-tax on the men. Scholars and Christian monks fled from the heathen barbarians, carrying to Europe their treasures and manuscripts. The time of mere destruction, however, was not long. The Scandinavians were practical men of affairs, and Norsemen and Danes had settled in Ireland for business. The "Great Island," as they called it, was a natural centre of their new world-wide commerce; lying within the trade circle formed by the ships that swept from the Orkneys and Hebrides round the Atlantic coast to the Loire and the Garonne, or that traversed the Irish Sea from Cantyre to Devonshire and Brittany. It was the shelter of voyaging ships, the recruiting ground of raiders, the winter-quarters of fleets; its commerce fell in naturally with the traffic of the western world. Danes and Irish were presently to the full as busy in trading as in fighting. Ireland became a commercial centre, a meeting place of the peoples. There came Grett with the Greek hat to buy captives for the Iceland market. A host of Saxons and Britons were brought over by Olaf and Ivar in 871. Almost every king of Norway sailed his fleet into Irish harbours, to drive off the rival Danish merchants, to broaden his traffic, to spy out some new store of gold, to load up with corn, to sweep the cattle down to the seashore for the "strand-hewing" that was to provision his crews with meat, fresh and salt, for their ocean course. Traders bargained then just as they bargain now. There is a harbour of Ardglass on the coast of County Down where a castle was built many centuries ago to protect the commerce of the port. The other day an Irishman repaired its ruins, and for a sign flew from it the flag of one of the Irish lords of the country, the Red Right Hand of O'Neill. At that very moment a light schooner sailed into the offing and at once flew in answer the Danish flag. The vessel was from Marsthal. Getting into port the crew bargained for herrings, counting out a hundred and ninety-five barrels of them by "chequers," while the Ardglass men checked the number on notched sticks. Neither knew one word of the other's tongue. So the Danes did business and sailed away, exactly as their forefathers had done a thousand years ago.

Between plundering and trading and marriages and alliances Norse and Irish got to know each other well, as we may see by the story of king Olaf Tryggwason and his dog. Olaf the Magnificent, most glorious and far-shining of sea-kings, famed beyond all others for the surpassing perfection of his warships, being married to Gytha sister of Olaf Kuaran king of Dublin, abode in England and occasionally in Ireland. "He happened once," says the Saga, "to be present in Ireland with a large naval force engaged in war. A foray to get stores being necessary, the men went on land and drove towards the shore a multitude of sheep and cattle; and there followed them a yeoman, who begged Olaf to give him back his cows from among the flock that they were driving off. King Olaf answered: 'Take your cows if you know them, and are able to separate them from the rest without delaying our journey; but, I think, neither you nor any other man can do that feat among so many hundred cattle as are in the drove.' The yeoman had a big cattle dog with him. So he sent the dog among the herd as they were driven off together, and the dog ran up and down among them all, and soon picked out and put aside as many of the man's cattle as in the yeoman's opinion were there. As these were all marked with one and the same mark, it was evident that the dog must have had a perfect knowledge of them. Then the King said: 'Wonderfully clever is your dog, yeoman; will you give him to me?' And the man answered: 'I will gladly do so.' Then the King straightway, in return, gave the yeoman a large gold bracelet, and promised him his friendship therewith. This dog, the best and most sensible of all dogs, was named Wigi, and Olaf had him for a long time afterwards." There came a day later when Olaf was entrapped by his enemies in the Baltic, sailing with his fleet on the far-famed Long Serpent—"never warship has been built in Northern lands its equal for beauty and size." "Right and proper is it," said Earl Eric, "that such a noble ship should belong to Olaf Tryggwason, for he is truly said to surpass other kings as much as the Long Serpent surpasses other ships." The King, with shield and helmet overlaid with gold, and red silken kirtle, stood on the ship's prow, a great dragon's head ornamented so that it seemed of gold, and when it gleamed far over the sea as the sun shone upon it, fear and terror were shot into men's hearts. "Lay the big ship more in front. My place in this warlike host is not at the back of all my men," he called. "I had the Serpent built of greater length than other ships that she might stretch the more boldly beyond them in the battle." The conflict of heroes raged long. As his enemies poured over the deck King Olaf, blood falling over his face and arm from under helmet and mail-sleeve, vanished, no man knew how, in the waters. The Long Serpent, sinking in the sea, was of no use to its conquerors. His queen was brought from under the deck weeping bitterly and so sore wounded with grief that she could neither eat nor drink, and died in nine days. Throughout the battle the dog Wigi lay without stirring before the castle of the Short Serpent; it carried him home along with Einar Thambaskelf, the youth of eighteen, hardest shooter of his time, who stood by the King in the Long Serpent, who when his own bow was broken stretched the King's beyond the arrow head and flung it away ("Too weak, too weak, the great King's bow"), who had sprung after the King into the water, and for his courage was given freedom by the victors. As they touched land Einar "before going on shore, went to the dog as he lay there, and said, 'We've no master now, Wigi!' At these words the dog sprang up growling, and with a loud yell, as if seized by anguish of heart, he ran on shore with Einar. There he went and lay down on the top of a mound, and would take no food from anyone, though he drove away other dogs, beasts and birds from what was brought to him. From his eyes, tears coursed one another down his nose, and thus bewailing the loss of his liege-lord, he lay till he died." From that day grief and sorrow lay on Einar. And men remembered the prophecy of the blind yeoman of Moster that in one voyage Norway should lose its four most noble things—the king, whose like had never been seen, the queen, best for sense and goodness that ever came into Norway, the greatest ship ever built in Norway, and the Irish dog, wiser and more clever than any other dog in the land.

In Ireland the power of the Scandinavians was shown in the foundation of two kingdoms, along the two main lines of sea traffic—Dublin on the eastern sea, and Limerick on the Atlantic. The Norwegian kingdom on the Liffey had its centre in the mound raised by the river-side for its Thing or Moot, near where the Dublin Parliament House rose nine hundred years later. The kingdom stretched over a narrow strip of shore, the memory of which was preserved for a thousand years, till a generation ago, in the jurisdiction of the Dublin Corporation over a long line of coast from the river Delvin below Drogheda to Arklow. Four fiords—Strangford and Carlingford to the north, and Wexford and Waterford to the south—lay outside the actual kingdom of Dublin, but were closely connected with it. Waterford kings were at times of the same family as the Dublin kings, and in the ninth and tenth centuries Waterford was sometimes independent and sometimes united to Dublin.

Dublin commanded a double line of commerce—from Scandinavia to Gaul, and by York to Novgorod and the Eastway. The kingdom was in close connection with the Danish kingdom of Northumbria, with its capital at York. For Danish Northumbria, opening on the North Sea by the Humber, formed the common meeting ground, the link which united the Northmen of Scandinavia and the Northmen of Ireland. A mighty confederation grew up. Members of the same house were kings in Dublin, in Man, and in York. Their descendants were among the chief settlers in Iceland. The Dublin kings married into the chief houses of Ireland, Scotland, and the Hebrides. The sea was the common highway which bound the powers together, and the sea was held by fleets of swift long-ships with from ninety to a hundred and fifty rowers or fighting men on board. The Irish Channel swarmed with ships of the Dublin kingdom. It became the mart of the Scandinavian traders, of Icelandic sailors, and men of Norway, and merchant princes landing from their cruise to sell their merchandise or their plunder. "You must this summer make a trading voyage," said Earl Hakon to his friend Thori Clack, "as is customary now with many, and go to Dublin in Ireland." Far-travelled traders carried from Dublin and York, deep into the inland of Russia, English coins and weapons and ornaments such as were used in Great Britain and Ireland.

"Limerick of the swift ships," looking out to the Atlantic and the Gaulish sea, was a rival even to Dublin. The Norwegians first fortified the town by an earthen or wooden fence, but presently by a wall of stone, "Limerick of the rivetted stones." Behind it lay a number of Norse settlements scattered over Limerick, Kerry, and Tipperary. The first settlers were from the Hebrides where Irishmen and Norse and Danes mingled as one people, interchanging names and mingling speech so that the Norse used Gaelic words for goblets for which they drank their wine, and the oats for their bread. The name *Maccus*, a later form of Magnus, was in the tenth century only used by the reigning families of Limerick, the Hebrides, and the Isle of Man. United by kinship and by trade, the lords of the Isles and the lords of Limerick constantly aided one another, and made joint expeditions. Once more the Gaulish trade was revived, and vessels sailed out from the Shannon to fetch wine and silks from the harbours of the Loire and the Garonne. From every bay and river-mouth between Waterford and Lough Foyle streams of commerce poured into the main current of the Atlantic trade. After a brief interruption in fact Ireland was once more in the ninth and tenth century in the full current of European life, and that in a double way. The lines of merchant vessels carried her trade, while the stream of her professors and scholars and missionaries brought her fame to every court in Europe.

King Ælfred has left his record of the three Irishmen who came "in a boat without oars from Hibernia, whence they had stolen away because for the love of God they would be on pilgrimage, they recked not where. The boat in which they fared was wrought of three hides and a half, and they took with them enough meat for seven nights." On the seventh day they drifted ashore at Cornwall, and were taken on to Ælfred whose captives they had thus become. Perhaps from them that great-hearted and far-sighted English king learned to honour the Irish. He sent gifts to monasteries in Ireland. He noted in his Chronicle the death of Suibhne, anchorite of Clonmacnois, "the most learned teacher among the Scots," said Ælfred.

From this story some may have supposed that the "primitive" Irishmen had not yet got beyond the rude fishing-boats of savage life. But we have here in fact only an instance of the strange contrasts which make Irish history so full of wonder, so rich in human interest. In the midst of a world of furious trade and war, Irish poets and mystics, obedient to the ancient message of their masters, still went down to the sea-brink abiding there "the revelation of knowledge." In the vast solitude of sea and sky beyond which, in which, waited the revelation, the seen and the unseen were confounded and limits of space and time fell away in infinity. The everlasting gates were there, the way of the soul's escape from imprisonment in shadows, the opening of the Eternal Reality. Abandoning will and fear, they cast themselves on Nature and the God immanent in Nature, and summoned by the silent call went out in faith, "they recked not where."

Thus in Ireland old worlds were ever intermixed with new. Pilgrims cast themselves on the sea in curraghs, and drifted to the Faroes and to Iceland carrying with them the power of piety and learning. But there were also Irish traders with business minds. They, like the French, learned from the Scandinavians to build ships, and like the French, used Norse words for their new sea-faring vessels, "brown-planked" warships, and merchant ships, ships large and small, and boats; and for the planks and sides, bottom-boards, row-benches, taff-rail, gunwale, the creaking, of the row-bench, the steersman. They learned too from the Scandinavians their method of raising a navy by dividing the country into districts, each of which had to equip and man so many ships which were to assemble at the summons to arms into the united war fleet—the levy and the fleet both called by Norse words. Sagas of the Danish time tell of "the fleet of the men of Munster," of "Munster of the swift ships," six or seven score of them ready to sail to Dundalk or to the Mull of Cantyre at the call of the king of Cashel.

The Irish had also their fleets of merchant ships. An old poem of about 900 A.D.gives a description of the dwellers on the coast from Carn or Mizen Head to Cork (the Irish clan of the O'Mahoneys chief among them)—

"High in beauty,
Whose resolve is quiet prosperity."

a description which has been generally considered quite unsuited to the Irish and more naturally reserved for Englishmen. The merchant princes won for their province the name of "Munster of the great riches." But the signs of foreign trade, chains and massive links of silver, and brooches of Scandinavia and the eastern world, are found all over Ireland—Belfast, Navan, Monaghan, Limerick, Galway, Cavan, King's and Queen's Counties—the patterns wholly unlike Irish work. There were enamelled glass beads, and silks and satins and stores of silver, oriental goods from the Caspian and East Mediterranean, which had been carried across Russia to Swedish and Danish lands and so to Ireland.

"What is best for a king?" asked an Irish poet of the tenth century.

"Fish in river-mouths.
Earth fruitful.
Inviting barks into harbour
Importing treasures from over-sea.
••••••
Silken raiment.
••••••
Abundance of wine and mead.
••••••
Let him foster every science."

Thus it was that the Irish wrested some advantage out of the Danish wars. They profited by the material skill and knowledge of the invaders. They were willing to absorb the foreigners, to marry with them, and even at times to share their wars. They learned from them to build ships, organise naval forces, advance in trade, and live in towns; they used Scandinavian words for the parts of a ship and the streets of a town. The Irish gave proof of a real national vigour. In outward and material civilization they accepted modern Norse methods, just as in our days the Japanese accepted modern Western inventions. But in what the Germans call Culture—in the ordering of society and law, of life and thought, the Irish like the Japanese never for a moment abandoned their national loyalty to their own country. During two centuries of Danish wars they did not loosen hold of their old civilization. "Concealing ancient lore, to hold any new thing fair," they said face to face with the new Scandinavian system, "this is the way of folly." They maintained their schools, their art and literature. They preserved their church. Writers of the ninth century describe the duty of an Irish king: he had to journey over the land and bring each chief under law: "let him enslave criminals": "let him perfect the proper due of every man of whatever is his on sea or land." On their side the tribes were to have for their protection not only "a lawful lord," but "a meeting of nobles"; "frequent assemblies"; "an assembly according to rules"; "a lawful synod." We read of yet larger Assemblies for the whole country "to make concord between the men of Ireland." If the chief places of the people were captured, they went out into the bog-lands to elect their kings according to their law. Thus when Cashel was held by the Danes the seventeen tribes of Munster gathered in a marshy glen, where the nobles sat in assembly on a mound, and decided to choose one Cennedig as king. But the queen, Cellachan's mother, appeared before them, and in a speech and a lay which she made declared the right of Cellachan. And when the champions of Munster heard these great words and the speech of the woman they rose up to make Cellachan king, "and gave thanks to the true magnificent God for having found him ... and put their hands in his hand, and placed the royal diadem round his head, and their spirits were raised at the grand sight of him."

Under the power of this national feeling the Irish learned from the Danes not only the new trade, but they learned also the new sea warfare, and understood their lesson so well that they were soon able to drive back the armies and fleets of the Danes, and to become themselves the leaders of Danish and Norse troops in war. It was about 950 A.D. that the Irish won their first famous naval victory. Cellachan, king of Cashel, had been taken prisoner by the Norse, and was carried to Sitric's ship at Dundalk. An army was sent from Munster across Ireland to rescue him. They demanded to have back their king. "Give honour to Cellachan in the presence of the men of Munster!" commanded Sitric in his wrath. "Let him even be bound to the mast! For he shall not be without pain in honour of them!" "I give you my word," said Cellachan, as he was lifted up, "that it is a greater sorrow to me not to be able to protect Cashel for you, than to be in great torture." "It is a place of watching where I am," he cried, high lifted above them all. "I see what your champions do not see, since I am at the mast of the ship." "Are these your ships that are coming now?" said he. For on the far horizon rose the masts of his fleet of Munster sailing into Dundalk harbour, six score of them, the full muster of the ships gathered from every sea port between Cork and Galway, from the regions of Bandon and Kinsale, from the land of the O'Driscolls who held the coast from Bandon across Clear harbour to Crookhaven and the river of Kenmare, from the Dingle peninsula, from "Kerry of the rushes" on the Shannon shore, from western Clare, and from Corcomroe and Burren. When the Irish captains looked on their king bound and fettered to the mast, their aspect became troubled, their colour changed, and their lips grew pale. From his place of agony Cellachan watched the onset of his sailors, and heard the rattle of swords and javelins filling the air, like the sound that arises from the seashore full of stones trodden by herds of cattle and racing horses. He saw the Irish fling tough ropes of hemp over the long prows of the Norse ships to hold them fast, while the Norsemen threw stout chains of blue iron. He saw his people, defended only by their "strong enclosures of linen cloth to protect bodies and necks and noble heads," as they dashed themselves into the Norse ships among the mail-clad warriors; he watched the heroic Failbe springing on the deck of Sitric's battle-ship, and with a high and deer-like leap mount on the mast, his right-hand sword swinging against the crowding enemy, while with the sword in his mighty left hand he cut the ropes that bound king Cellachan. In the moment of his king's salvation Failbe fell dead. As the Norsemen struck off his head and set it upon the prow of the ship, Failbe's foster-brother, mad for revenge, with an eager falcon-like leap sprang into the warship, and since no weapon of his could pierce the armour of the Norse king, he fixed his white hands in the bosom of Sitric's coat of mail and dragged him down into the water, so that they together reached the gravel and the sand of the sea and rested there. After six hours' battle the remnant of the Scandinavian fleet put out to sea, and, says the old saga, they carried neither King nor Chieftain with them.

After that battle came other triumphs; the fleet of the kings of Ailech that carried off plunder and booty from the Hebrides: Brian Boru's expedition of the Norsemen of Dublin, Waterford, Wexford, and of the men of

Munster, and of almost all of the men of Erin such of them as were fit to go to sea, and they levied tribute from Saxons and Britons as far as the Clyde and Argyle. The spirit of independence rose high, and victorious warriors established again the rule of the Irish in their own land.

But the Danes had no mind to let Ireland and her harbours and her sea routes fall out of their hands. The great conflict of the two peoples came about sixty years after the victory of Cellachan.

The Danes had now held command of the sea for two hundred years. About 1000 A.D., in the glory of success, their kings, like later monarchs in Europe, began to think of their "Imperial Destiny." It seemed time to perfect the whole business and round off the borders of their State. So Swein Forkbeard of Denmark proposed to create a Scandinavian Empire which should extend from the Slavic shores of the Baltic to the rim of the Atlantic, with the North Sea as a lake of this wide dominion. Swein overran England, and his son Cnut ruled from the Baltic to the Irish Channel, lord of Denmark, Norway, England, and the Danes of Dublin (for he minted coins even there), with London as the chief city of the new Danish Empire. The imperial plan was not yet complete. Danish rule was to extend to the outermost land on the Atlantic. But Ireland blocked the way. The Ireland of King Brian Boru—of men who lived (as they said) "on the ridge of the world," men bred in the free air of the plains and the mountains and the sea—left the Scandinavian Empire with a ragged edge on the line of the Atlantic commerce. In the spring of 1014 the Danish army gathered in the Bay of Dublin to straighten out the boundaries of the Empire on the western Ocean. There met a mighty host under the "Black Raven" of the pagans, woven with heathen spells; "when the wind blew out the banner it was as though the Raven flapped his wings for flight." In that Imperial army there were warriors "from all the west of Europe," from Iceland, the Orkneys, the Baltic Islands, from Norway a thousand men in ringed armour, from Northumbria two thousand pagans, "not a villain of them who had not polished armour of iron or brass encasing their bodies from head to foot." On the night before the battle Woden himself, the old god of war, rode up through the dusk men said, on a dapple-grey horse, halbert in hand, to take counsel with his champions.

But Woden's last fight was come. The full tide of the morning carried the pagan host over the level sands to the landing at Clontarf. The army of King Brian Boru lay before them. From sunrise to sunset on Good Friday that desperate battle raged, the hair of the warriors flying in the wind, says the old chronicler, as thick as the sheaves floating in a field of oats. The Scandinavian scheme of a Northern Empire was shattered on that day, when with the evening flood-tide the remnant of the Danish host put out to sea. The work which had been begun by the fleet of Cellachan in Dundalk harbour sixty-four years before, was completed by Brian Boru where the Liffey opens into the Bay of Dublin. For a hundred, and fifty years to come Ireland kept its independence. England was once again, as in the time of the Roman dominion, made part of a continental empire. Ireland, as in the days of Rome, still lay outside the new imperial system.

Clontarf marked the passing of an old age, the beginning of a new. We may see the advent of the new men in the names of adventurers that landed with the Danes on that low shore at Clontarf—the first great drops of the coming storm. There were lords from Normandy, Eoghan Barun or John the Baron, and Richard, with another, perhaps Robert of Melun. There was Goistilin Gall, a Frenchman from Gaul. There was somewhere about that time Walter the Englishman, a leader of mercenaries from England. In such names we see the heralds of the approaching change. A revolution in the fortunes of the world had in fact opened. Scandinavian pre-eminence on the sea was even now passing away, as that of the Frisians had passed away two hundred years before. New lords of commerce seized the traffic of sea and land when the Normans, "citizens of the world," carried their arms and their cunning from the Moray Firth to the Straits of Messina, from the Seine to the Euphrates. The Teutonic peoples that now girded the North Sea—Normans, Germans of the Hanseatic League, English—were to supersede Danes and Norwegians. Trade moreover had once more spread over the high roads of Europe, as in the days of the Roman Empire, and the peoples of the south, Italians and Gauls, had taken up again their ancient commerce.

In the new commerce as in the old Ireland was to take her full part. The island lay in the moving life that stirred the great seas, washed by that whirlpool of activity. From every shore she saw the sails of busy traffickers bearing the commerce of the known world, and carrying too its thought and art. The people had not lost their wit. They shared in the enterprise and the profit of the new commerce. The great routes were open, from Scandinavia to Gaul, and down the Irish Channel. The Danish traffic across England was not forgotten, and as the trade of the German coasts developed, busier lines of commerce were opened from the Irish harbours of the south eastward to the North Sea and the Baltic.

It is an unfinished tale I tell. But it may remind us of one gift of Nature to Ireland—the freedom of Europe by the sea. We have seen the dim figures of the flint-men, the Bronze-men, the first Gaels, reaching out hands to Scandinavia and to the Mediterranean lands. We have seen Ireland on the borders of the Roman Empire, free and unconquered, busy in trade, busier still in learning, carrying across the Gaulish Sea treasures of classical knowledge. Again Ireland appeared when the barbarians had spread over Europe, still unconquered, sending back across the Ocean the learning she had stored up, the free distributor on the Continent of the classics and science and Christian teaching. We have seen the island again on the fringe of the Scandinavian Empire, even now unconquered, and still in the mid-stream of European traffic. When a new revolution came, and trade swelled under the Normans, every Irish port was full. Irishmen sailed every sea. Their fabrics were sold in every country as far as Russia and Naples. Through the long centuries they never lost the habit of the sea and of Europe. In the middle ages Spanish coin was almost the chief currency in Ireland, so great was the Irish trade with Spain; and in the eighteenth century the country was still full of Spanish, Portuguese, and French money in daily use—the moydore, the doubloon, the pistole, the Louis d'or, the new Portuguese gold coin. So much so that in the Peninsular war Ireland was ransacked for foreign coins to send to the army in Spain and Portugal.

But that story is over. Ireland at last was swept within the orbit of an Empire—not as a free member of a federation, but in full subjection, with every advantage that complete military and police control could afford. Natural geography gave place to political geography, and the way of the Empire ruled out the way of the sea. "I should not presume," wrote Richard Cox, Esquire, Recorder of Kinsale, in dedicating to their Majesties William and Mary a History of Ireland from the Conquest thereof, which he printed at St. Paul's Churchyard in 1689. "I should not presume to lay this treatise at your Royal feet, but that it concerns a noble Kingdom, which is one of the most considerable branches of your mighty Empire.

"It is of great Advantage to it, that it is a Subordinate Kingdom of the Crown of *England*; for it is from that Royal Fountain that the Streams of Justice, Peace, Civility, Riches and all other Improvements have been derived to it; so that the Irish are (as Campion says) beholding to God for being conquered.

"And yet Ireland has been so blind in this Great Point of its true Interest, that the Natives have managed almost a continual war with the English ever since the first Conquest thereof; so that it has cost your Royal Predecessors an unspeakable mass of Blood and Treasure to preserve it in true Obedience.

"But no cost can be too great where the Prize is of such value; and whoever considers the Situation, Ports, Plenty, and other Advantages of Ireland will confess, that it must be retained at what rate soever; because if it should come into an Enemy's Hands, England would find it impossible to *flourish*; and perhaps difficult to *subsist*without it.

"To demonstrate this assertion, it is enough to say that Ireland lies in the *Line of Trade*, and that all the English vessels that sail to the *East*, *West* and *South*, must, as it were, run the *gauntlet* between the Harbours of Brest and Baltimore: and I might add that the Irish Wool, being transported, would soon ruine the English clothing Manufacture.

"Hence it is that all Your Majesties Predecessors have kept close to this Fundamental Maxim, of retaining Ireland inseperably united to the Crown of England."

The house of Hanover ended what the Tudors had begun. Ireland became an island beyond an island. But the great deep still gives to the country an abiding unity. In ancient days the Irish had a noble figure by which they proclaimed the oneness of the land within its Ocean bounds. The three waves of Erin they said, smote upon the shore with a foreboding roar when danger threatened the island. One wave called to Munster at an inlet of Cork; two of them sounded in Ulster, at the mouth of the Bann and in the bay of Dundrum. The Ocean bore the same fate to Munster and to Ulster. And in fact so long as the sea surrounds this island, so long all its peoples must be linked in a common fortune. The deep that encompasses Ireland has made this country one, gathering together into the Irish family all races that have entered within its circuit. By the might of that encircling Ocean the men of Ireland are bound together in one inheritance, unchanging amid ceaseless change.

CHAPTER III

A GREAT IRISH LADY

WE are often told that the civilization of a people is marked by the place of its women: a rule by which the Irish stand high. In the fifteenth century, as at all times, their annals record many noble ladies "distinguished for knowledge, hospitality, good sense and piety"; "humane and charitable"; "a nurse to all guests and strangers, and to all the learned men in Ireland." Of these Margaret, daughter of O'Carroll lord of Ely, wife of Calvagh O'Connor Faly lord of Offaly (lands which lie across the boundaries of the modern King's and Queen's Counties and Kildare), was the most illustrious. She came of a learned race. The O'Carrolls, in the course of little more than a century (1253-1373), held the See of Cashel for sixty years; and O'Carroll had been Archbishop of

Tuam; and Margaret's father, lord of Ely, was "the general patron of all the learned men of Ireland." "This Teige was deservedly a man of greate accompt and fame with the professors of Poetrye and Musicke of Ireland and Scotland, for his liberality extended towards them, and every of them in generalle." So highly was he esteemed among the chiefs that he was forbidden by the Irish captains of east Munster to carry out his wish of resigning his lordship of Ely (1396). He made a pilgrimage, however, that year to the threshold of the apostles, with his companions O'Brien, Gerald, and Thomas Calvagh MacMurchadh of the royal race of Leinster; and coming back through England visited Richard II. at Westminster, who received him graciously, and being then about to cross to Calais for his marriage with Isabella of France, and the conclusion of a treaty of peace with the French king, invited O'Carroll to accompany him in his retinue. Ten years later he was slain by the English, the boy-prince Thomas of Lancaster, son of Henry IV., being then Viceroy in Ireland, and under him the Lord Deputy Scrope. The English army fell on him unawares at Callan; for whose death indeed the sun stood still, said their account, to light the Deputy and the fierce Prior of Kilmainham in the evening surprise and the six miles' ride of slaughter, where eight hundred, or some said three thousand, of his people fell. Some time after the massacre Margaret married the most successful leader in his day of the Irish, Calvagh O'Connor Faly, son of Murchadh, the "Lord of Offaly, of the cattle-abounding land," descended from Conchobar of the race of Cathair Mór, King of Leinster. Brought up amid the perils and sorrows of constant war, her fortunes were now transferred to a country where the conflict with the English knew no interlude. To understand her story it is necessary to show very briefly the situation of Offaly.

The land of the O'Connors adjoined that of the O'Carrolls under the Slieve Bloom mountains. The old Offaly, from Sliabh-Bladhma, now Slieve Bloom, to the hill of Alenn, and from Sliabh-Cualann in Wicklow to the Great Heath, is a plain as level as a tranquil sea. On its western side a long low ridge north of Slieve Bloom had given shelter to the two St. Sinchealls; a church had risen by the holy well; and the fair-town of Killeigh on "the field of the long ridge," profiting by the traffic from the Shannon to the Liffey. There Murchadh O'Connor founded for the Franciscans a monastery (1393) said to be the third in size and importance of the monasteries of Ireland, the burial place of his race. In what was once the Abbey churchyard, tombstones of the O'Doynes, deeply sculptured with their armorial bearings, recall a great family of Offaly. On the eastern side of Offaly Norman settlers had pushed back the boundary from the Dublin hills to Rathangan, where a strong fort and church stood at the head of the plain through which the Barrow and the Slaney flowed south to Waterford and Wexford; and on that important trade route Thomas O'Connor Faly had founded a Franciscan monastery (1302), under the walls of Hugh de Lacy's fort at Castledermot. To the north lay Meath—"cemetery of the valourous Gael"—whose colonists had incessant war with Offaly. It was a land over which the earliest Norman settlers had swept from de Lacy's fort of Castledermot to that of Durrow; a land which was again the chief centre of struggle when the Irish attack drove the English power back to the plains of Meath, and which in the renewed wars of the English under the Tudors became the scene of ferocious reprisals and calculated obliteration of its race and name. From Calvagh's first battle all his fighting was on the plains of Meath. Once he made a raid in the land of the O'Mores; and when his sons grew up they had disputes with Irish neighbours. But the only war of Calvagh from 1385 to 1458 was a war against the English.

The family were bitter Irreconcilables; since the days of an older Calvagh, the "Great Rebel," who a hundred years before (1307), had been invited with thirty of the Offaly chiefs to dine at Castle-Carberry on Trinity Sunday with "the treacherous baron," Sir Pierce Bermingham, the "Hunter of the Irish"; and were deceitfully murdered, the Great Rebel and all, as they rose from table. This new Calvagh fought the invaders for over sixty years, from youth to old age, with scarcely a pause—a man of humour as well as courage. Once when the English troops with their Irish followers had ridden to the very borders of Killeigh (1406)—the religious and business centre of Offaly—Calvagh with half a dozen horsemen came upon a body of plundering kerns, one carrying off on his back a great cauldron which Calvagh had lent his friend MacMaoilcorra for brewing beer. "There is your caldron with the kerns," cried MacMaoilcorra helplessly, "take it and discharge me of my loan."

"I accept of it where it is," mocked Calvagh, and flung "the shot of a stone" which hit the cauldron straight, at the great noise and report whereof the plunderers cast away their spoil and fled in consternation. In the great rout of the English that day the Irish won back from them the chiefest relic of Connacht, the cap or mitre of S. Patrick stolen from Elphin.

In Calvagh's days the Irish revival had pushed back the rule of Dublin Castle to a strip of coast land some twenty miles by thirty. There flew a tale of panic (1385) that the Irish "were confederate with Spain," and that "at this next season, as is likely, there will be made a conquest of the greater part of the land." Revenue was falling, English colonists were flying across the water, and prayers for help were sent over to the English king. The king's favourite De Vere, appointed Marquis of Dublin and Duke of Ireland (1386), got no farther than Wales, and English pretentions over the island under a confused series of shifting rulers became the mock of Europe. Stung by the taunt that he who desired to be made head of the Holy Roman Empire could not even subdue Ireland, Richard II. made his fantastic journey across the Irish Channel (1394), carrying a wardrobe of untold cost in which one jewelled coat alone was worth thirty thousand marks, and with a following of four thousand squires and thirty thousand archers, a greater army, some said, than Edward III. commanded at Crecy. Thus Calvagh had the rare opportunity of seeing the arrival in Ireland of the only king of England who landed there in the five hundred years between the coming of Henry II. and John (1171 and 1210), and that of James II. (1689)—all four driven over by personal necessities, not by any concern whatever for the Irish people or their well-being. The English troops were flung back from the O'Connor land and from Ely of the O'Carrolls, with many men slain and many horses captured, and fresh supplies were sent for from England. But Richard, unlike any other king that visited Ireland, was moved by the spirit of the country. The temper he had shown thirteen years before in the Peasant Revolt—"I am your King and Lord, good people; what will ye?"—manifested itself again amid the troubles of his Irish lordship. To the Irish people he showed the first signs of sympathy and respect. Laying aside the hostile banners of England, he substituted the golden cross and silver birds of his patron saint, Edward the Confessor—the only King of England reported to have any connection with an Irish house, if as some historians say (on what evidence I do not know) his Queen's sister Driella was wife of O'Brien, king of Munster. "To Us and our Council," he wrote to England, "it appears that the Irish rebels have rebelled in consequence of the injustice and grievances practised towards them, for which they have been afforded no redress." Peace was made with "his rebel MacMorrough"; and treaties signed with the chiefs, seventy-five of them, were sent to England in two hampers, while Richard returned to Westminster leaving Roger Mortimer, heir to the throne, as Viceroy. The next year, as we have seen, he received O'Carroll of Ely at his palace with especial honour.

With his disappearance the policy of peace and reform came to an end. The meaning of Mortimer's rule was clear to the Irish. He claimed by inheritance of Lionel Duke of Clarence, son of Edward III., to be Earl of Ulster, Lord of Connacht, Trim, Leix, and Ossory, thus threatening the Ulster chiefs with a war of conquest, and the lord of Offaly and the middle Irish with the complete encircling of their lands, their isolation and destruction. Edmund Mortimer, son-in-law of Clarence, had already appeared as Viceroy (1380-1381), carrying with him the sword adorned with gold "which had belonged to the good king Edward" the Confessor, and his great bed of black satin embroidered with the arms of de Mortimer and Ulster: he sent much spoil and cattle to England, and died in the midst of his warfare. His son Roger was appointed Viceroy (1382-1383) a boy of ten; and orders were sent to arrest all those who by land or water should send or sell horses, salt, armour, iron, gold, silver, corn, or other provisions, to any of the Irish. Once more this same Roger Mortimer was Viceroy in 1395, riding to war for his inheritance in the dress and arms of an Irish chief. Calvagh captured the earl of Kildare who was held to ransom by his father; and the Carlow men routed and slew the young Mortimer himself (1398). On which Richard sent over his half-brother, the Duke of Surrey (1398), and already forgetful of his Irish compacts of three years before, granted his favourite lands which by treaty belonged to MacMurchadh. When war naturally followed the king proposed to subdue the Irish by a new visit (1399), this time forsaking the tradition of the Confessor for that of Henry II., and bearing the royal regalia of England and the miraculous consecrated oil of St. Thomas of Canterbury used at coronations. Chanting a last collect with the canons of St. George he set sail for Waterford, bringing with him the Duke of Lancaster (afterwards Henry v.) a boy of twelve years, to take his first lesson in war. The army was set to fell MacMurchadh's woods; a space was cleared, villages and houses set on fire, and in that scene Richard made the young Henry knight, even while the Duke of Lancaster was landing in Yorkshire to seize the English crown. Before July closed the betrayed king had hurried back to England, there to meet his death of horror.

So ended the royal dream of chivalry in Ireland, as it had closed before in England. Whatever imaginative feeling for the Irish, whatever memories of their old tradition or visions of a reconciliation of the two civilizations, had stirred Richard ii., these disappeared under the Lancastrian kings. Stern conquest was their creed, as soon as their wars in England, Wales, Scotland, and France would allow it.

The comings and goings of English governors in Ireland during the French wars read like the wanderings of the Wiking raiders, now on the Irish side of the sea, now on the French, as the chances of campaign might open the best prospects of adventure, plunder and ransom. Viceroys, deputies, lords justices, of a summer or two, each with his twelve months' policy of extortion, slaughter, and vain treaties, headed brief marches and skirmishes, campaigned on the plan that there was never a battle to be opened on a Monday or after noonday, hunted or purchased prisoners not for their defeat but for their ransom, and in succession sailed away for the better ventures of the French war. "The most cause of destruction," the English colonists declared to the king in 1435, arose because "during thirty years past the Lieutenants and other Governors did not come here but for a sudden journey or a hosting." As their power shrank their salaries and armies were increased. Governors no longer pretended to control the war, but returning to the lawless practice of the first adventurers, ordered any man who could to go out and fight however and wherever he pleased; and the lords about Dublin, freed from all restraints of law, kept troops of horse and foot against "Irish enemies," "English rebels," and their own personal foes.

The Lieutenant sent by Henry IV. to rule Ireland (1401) was his son Thomas of Lancaster twelve years old; and the first in a series of changing deputies Sir Stephen Scrope, an old soldier trained in French and Flemish wars, and as ready to serve Henry as Richard. He it was who slew O'Carroll, Richard's friend; and against him Murchadh and Calvagh O'Connor warred victoriously in Meath (1406, 1408). The prior of Kilmainham being deputy (who had also been on that ride of death when the sun stood still), the O'Connors captured the sheriff of Meath (1411) and took a great price for his ransom. The three months' rule of Sir John Stanley (1413) first governor of Henry V. was ended by his death after the curse of the chief bard Niall O'Higgin whom he had plundered at Usnach—"the second poetical miracle" of this famous bard. In vain his successor Archbishop Cranley, whose eighty years alone held him back from battle, gathered his clergy at Castledermot to pray for English victory: O'Connor and MacGeoghagan routed the English, and held to ransom prisoners for two thousand six hundred marks besides other fines (1414). Sir John Talbot Lord Furnival followed (1414), hovering between Ireland, England, and France—to the English "an ancient fox and politique captain," to the French "a very scourge and daily terror," to the Irish "a son of curses for his venom and a devil for his evil." He called out the troops to active war, slew many rebels, and gave protection to neither saint nor sanctuary; it was his policy to "oblige one Irish enemy to serve upon the other," by forcing defeated chiefs to swear that they would fight under him against their countrymen. Still the O'Connors raided Meath for arms, horses, and prisoners (1417). Calvagh was once treacherously captured by a Meath lord, from whom Talbot in hope of a ransom purchased him; but the prisoner escaped that same night. To Talbot succeeded (1420) James the White Earl of Ormond, back from the French wars. Precepts drawn up to guide his conduct declared that as "the Irish are false by kind, it were expedient and a charity to execute upon them wilful and malicious transgressors the king's laws somewhat sharply." He too had been at the death of O'Carroll, and once again, it was said, the sun miraculously stood still for three hours, and no pit or bog annoyed horse or man on his part, while he slaughtered the Irish on "the red moor of Athy." Twice every week the clergy of Dublin went in solemn procession praying for his good success against those disordered persons which now in every quarter of Ireland had degenerated to their old trade of life, and repined at the English. The colonists petitioned Henry v. that he would induce the Pope to proclaim a holy crusade against the Irish, "in perpetual destruction of those enemies." It was in the bitterness of this exasperated conflict that Murchadh O'Connor Faly won a last victory (1421), before he laid down arms and entered his monastery of Killeigh to die —"Murchadh of the defeats."

For thirty-seven years Calvagh now led his people's fight against "the English manner of government," in other words, the destruction of the Irish. He seized more lords and officers, won more wealth, and recovered more Irish territory than any lord in Leinster. At this time the Desmonds, out of favour under Lancastrian kings, had withdrawn to Munster to build up their dominion in the south, while the Ormonds and their cousins and rivals the Talbots fought for power. Passing strangers appeared in Dublin Castle; but with occasional interruptions the actual authority swung back, now to Ormond and his half-brother the prior of Kilmainham, now to Talbot and his brother the Archbishop of Dublin, till each family had held the chief control many times. The Talbots stood for pure English rule, and excelled in severity alike towards colonists and natives. They used for their wars and their rewards Irish taxes, coyn and livery; but at Westminster they represented Ormond's iniquity in levying the like taxes, and his faint and wavering sympathies for his countrymen, as treason of the darkest hue; his favouring his Irish friends, keeping Irish soldiers for his following, letting lands slip into Irish hands, making Irishmen knights of the shire; with a few additions thrown in of his sloth, violence, and corruption—"courses ruinous and destructive" to the English. In the midst of this discord Calvagh seems to have leaned to Ormond. His wife, apparently by a friendly arrangement, was given tribute from an Ormond lordship in Kildare. He himself held Talbot's cousin Thomas to ransom in his prison at Killeigh: he took "blackrent" or tribute from the English of Meath.

Meanwhile both Ulster and Offaly were set aflame by the coming of a new Mortimer Viceroy (1423) Edmund, son of Roger of the Irish dress. When he landed with an English army O'Neill and O'Donnell had already marched over Louth and Meath (1423), compelling the English to give hostages and guarantees for their pledge that they would be under tribute for ever. Edmund called O'Neill and some of the leaders to his Trim Castle, and made arrangements with him; but they had scarcely left when he died of plague (1424), and Talbot, then Lord Chief Justice, pursued the chiefs and carried them prisoners to Dublin, demanding hostages and ransom. Calvagh on his side raided Meath, where he seized the Marshal of the English army, the Seneschal of the Viceroy's manor, and other squires. But it was now the turn of Ormond, who had lately come to Ireland bringing a host of Saxons, and adding great strength to the English wars; and Talbot made terms with Calvagh before the appointment of the new viceroy. But the peace was brief. Calvagh entered into alliance with the princes of Ulster. He married his daughter Finola to O'Donnell, "harrasser and destroyer of the English." And when O'Neill with O'Donnell marched a great army to Mullingar (1431), and on the Moat where O'Melaghlin had in old times ruled and judged Leinster, gathered the chiefs to take his wages and acknowledge him leader for the war, Calvagh joined his host in the ravaging of Westmeath till the English paid a heavy price for the sparing of their country. Later, when his son-in-law O'Donnell was captured and imprisoned in Dublin Castle (1434), then sent to England (1435), and finally to the Isle of Man (1439) to die there in prison, Calvagh marched, year after year, through Meath to avenge his captivity. The Justiciary or Deputy himself was taken prisoner by Calvagh's son, and kept some time till the English of Dublin ransomed him. In the feuds of the barons he found allies. The son of MacFheorais, chief of the Berminghams and heir of "the treacherous baron," suffered "an abuse" in the great court of Trim, the Governor's castle. For as he entered the court (1443) under the safeguard of Ormond, the son of Barnewell, Treasurer of Meath, beat a *Caimin*—namely, a stroke of his finger on the nose of Bermingham's son. On which he stole out of the town, and went towards O'Connor Faly, and they joined together, and it is hard to know that ever was such abuse better revenged than the said Caimin. They burned and preyed Meath and obtained their full demands—that Calvagh should have his duties from the English during his life as Lord of his territory, and that the Clan-Feorais should have all their hostages freely restored; and not only that but they obtained in this "war of Caimin" all conditions such as they demanded for holding peaceable quiet with the English. Ever more formidable, Calvagh now led his kerns to Moyclare beyond Maynooth and to Tara itself (1446). Talbot, made Earl of Shrewsbury, was called back from the French wars. He re-built Castle Carberry, the castle of the old massacre, to defend Meath against Berminghams and O'Connors, caused Calvagh to make peace, to ransom his son taken in the wars, and deliver many beeves for the royal kitchen; and made a statute (1447) that English and Irish should no more be confounded together by their dress, but that every Englishman who did not shave in the English manner once at least in two weeks, should be treated as an Irish enemy—a statute which survived till the reign of Charles I. His last characteristic outrage was the treacherous capture of Felim O'Reilly who had gone to Trim at his own invitation, and the like deceitful seizing of the Savadges. Talbot seems to have been distinguished for his violated pledges among the crowd of English officials whose broken faith became a byword. "Thy safe-guarding," said the poet, "I confide to God; to Mary's sweet and only Son; that He may shelter thee from Anglo-word of Englishmen, and from the gentiles' act of violence." The prisoners all died in Trim Castle, disappointing the Viceroy of his ransom. After which Talbot disappeared for the last time to France (1447), followed by the curses of the Irish—"the learned say there came not from the time of Herod anyone so wicked in evil deeds." In his stead came Richard Plantagenet, Duke of York, heir to the English crown, and to all the earldoms and lordships of the Mortimers.

No doubt the race of O'Connor Faly was a family of irreconcilables; men fighting honourably to defend their land and people, each leader of them in his turn strong to obtain "great rewards from the English for making peace with them, as had been usual with his predecessors." They were the sort of people for whom Dublin Castle for a hundred years past, and many hundred years to come, had but one name, "the Irish enemy," ever bitterly complaining of the "mere Irish, men that are truly beastly and ignorant," living under "the wicked and damnable law called Brehon Law," "which by reason ought not to be named a law, but an evil custom."

There was a good deal however that Dublin Castle did not know or care to know. In the midst of this desolating war the story of Margaret, wife of O'Connor, gives us a glimpse into the life of the Irish clans behind the fastnesses that screened them from English view. It might seem that amid centuries of conflict, ever-present danger, preyings and raidings, statutes to shut them out from learning, trade, or advancement in their church, and torrents of slander to defile their name, the Irish might in truth have fallen into the nomad barbarism and the beastly ignorance of which they were accused by the English from that time to this. In fact however the people, endowed with an immense vitality, were busily occupied with commerce and with learning. Irish princes were lively competitors with the English merchants of the Pale. In all their territories the places of fairs were thronged with dealers, English and Irish, who did business together in peace and amity, while profits poured into Irish coffers. English statutes forbade any Englishman to deal in an Irish market: English merchants therefore put on Irish dress, rode on Irish saddles, talked Irish, and went on trading as before. Towns and monasteries of the colonists forced from the government charters allowing them to traffic with Irish dealers. The O'Connors lay at the meeting point of natural trade-routes, with their fair-town at Killeigh, and their establishments at Rathangan and Castledermot; and Margaret was a patron of commerce, as she was of learning and religion. "She was the only woman," the Annals tell us, "that has made the most of repairing the highways and erecting bridges, churches, and Mass books, and of all manner of things profitable to serve God and her soul, and while the world stands her many gifts to the Irish and Scottish nations shall never be numbered."

She was a patron too of the schools of the learned, which under the Irish revival had sprung into new and vigorous life, training students in every corner of Ireland, and sending out scholars to all the universities of Europe. "The company that read all books, they of the church and of the poets both: such of these as shall be perfect in knowledge, forsake not thou their intimacy ever"—this, according to an Irish poet, was the high duty of chiefs, of the noble and wealthy; and Margaret was faithful to the tradition of her people. Her friendship for the learned, the royal magnificence of her bounty was long remembered in Ireland. The year 1433 was a year of trouble. Ormond ravaged the land of Ely and destroyed the fortresses of the O'Carrolls. Margaret's daughter Finola —"the most beautiful and stately, the most renowned and illustrious woman of her time, her own mother only excepted," blessed with "the blessing of guests and strangers, of poets and philosophers"—only saved Tirconail from the enemies of O'Neill and of MacDonnell and his Scots by herself going, after the fashion of the strong-hearted and independent women of Ireland, to meet them at Inishowen, and there "made peace without leave from O'Donnell." It was a year terribly named in Irish tradition, "'the summer of slight acquaintance,' because no one used to recognise friend or relative," for the greatness of the famine that lay on the land. Such was the time of Margaret's great benevolence. "It is she that twice in one year proclaimed to and commonly invited (*i.e.*, in the dark days of the year, to wit, on the feast day of Da Sinchell [26 March] in Killachy), all persons, both Irish and Scottish, or rather Albaines, to two general feasts of bestowing both meat and moneys, with all manner of gifts, whereunto gathered to receive gifts the matter of two thousand and seven hundred persons, besides gamesters and poor men, as it was recorded in a Roll to that purpose, and that accompt was made thus, *ut vidimus*—viz., the chief *kins* of each family of the learned Irish was by Gilla-na-naemh MacÆgan's hand, the chief Judge to O'Connor, written in the Roll, and his adherents and kinsmen, so that the aforesaid number of 2,700 was listed in that Roll with the Arts of *Dan*, or poetry, Music, and Antiquity. And Maelin O'Maelconry, one of the chief learned of Connacht, was the first written in that Roll, and first paid and dieted, or set to supper, and those of his name after him, and so forth every one as he was paid he was written in that Roll, for fear of mistake, and set down to eat afterwards. And Margaret on the garrots of the great church of Da Sinchell clad in cloth of gold, her dearest friends about her, her clergy and Judges too. Calvagh himself on horseback by the church's outward side, to the end that all things might be done orderly, and each one served successively. And first of all she gave two chalices of gold as offerings that day on the Altar to God Almighty, and she also caused to nurse or foster too [two] young orphans. But so it was, we never saw nor heard neither the like of that day nor comparable to its glory and solace. And she gave the second inviting proclamation (to every one that came not that day) on the feast day of the Assumption of our Blessed Lady Mary in harvest, at or in the Rath-Imayn, and so we have been informed that that second day in Rath-Imayn was nothing inferior to the first day."

We know something of the manner of these national festivals, for the Irish were long practised in the organizing of general conventions, and their poets have left us some curious details. One tells of a company of the Tyrone poets gathered in 1577 at O'Neill's house, where the poets sat ranged along a hall hung with red on either side of the chief, and standing up beside the host pledged him in ale quaffed from golden goblets and beakers of horn; and having told their song or story for a price, took their gifts of honour. Another describes a greater company, such an assembly as that of Margaret, invited in 1351 to the castle of William O'Kelly.

"The chroniclers of comely Ireland, it is a gathering of a mighty host, the company is in the town; where is the street of the chroniclers?

"The fair, generous-hearted host have another spacious avenue of white houses for the bardic companies and the jugglers.

•••••••

"Such is the arrangement of them, ample roads between them; even as letters in their lines.

"Each thread of road, bare, smooth, straight, firm, is contained within two threads of smooth, conical roofed houses.

"The ridge of the bright-furrowed slope is a plain lined with houses, behind the crowded plain is a fort, as it were a capital letter."

The castle itself was worthy of one born into the Irish inheritance, of the great lineage of their race: far off it is recognised, the star-like mass of stone, its outer smoothness like vellum—a castle which was the standard of a mighty chieftain; bright is the stone thereof, ruddy its timber.

"Close is the joining of its timber and its lime-washed stone; there is no gaping where they touch; the work is a triumph of art.

"There is much artistic ironwork upon the shining timber: on the smooth part of each brown oaken beam workmen are carving animal figures.

"On the smooth wall of the warm mansion—amazing in its beauty—is the track of a slender, pointed pen; light, fresh, narrow.

"The bardic companies of pleasant-meadowed Fóla, and those of Scotland—a distant journey—will be acquainted with one another after arriving in William's lofty castle.

"Herein will come the seven grades who form the shape of genuine poesy; the seven true orders of poets, their entrance is an omen of expenditure.

"Many coming to the son of Donnchadh from the north, no less from the south, an assembly of scholars: a billeting from west and east, a company seeking for cattle.

"There will be jurists, of legal decisions; wizards, and good poets; the authors of Ireland, those who compose the battle rolls, will be in his dwelling.

"The musicians of Ireland—vast the flock—the followers of every craft in general, the flood of companies, side by side—the tryst of all is to one house.

"In preparation for those who come to the house there has been built—it is just to boast of it—according to the desire of the master of the place, a castle fit for apple-treed Emain.

"There are sleeping booths for the company, wrought of woven branches, on the bright surface of the pleasant hills.

"The poets of the Irish land are prepared to seek O'Kelly. A mighty company is approaching his house, an avenue of peaked hostels is in readiness for them.

"Hard by that—pleasant is the aspect—a separate street has been appointed by William for the musicians, that they may be ready to perform before him.

"This lofty tower opposite to us is similar to the Tower of Breoghan, from which the best of spears were cast; from which Ireland was perceived from Spain.

"By which the mighty progeny of Mil of Spain—a contentious undertaking—contested the land with sharp spear points, so that they became men of Ireland.

•••••••

"From Greece to fair Spain, from Spain to Ireland, such the wanderings of the mighty progeny of Mil, the host of the seasoned, finely wrought weapons."

Such was the assembly, "the mound of grand convention," to which Margaret invited Irish scholars. In such national festivals the passion of war was exchanged for a nobler pride of life. The chief recognised his place in the wide commonwealth of the Gaelic people. Each one of the company of scholars was reminded that whatever lord he served, Ireland was his country and the fortunes of the race his care. And the people themselves, sharing the festivities of those joyous assemblies, and entertained by the best that Ireland could give of music and literature, could still exult through their successive generations in the kinship of the whole race, Irish and Scots. Irishmen to-day may remember that the scholars gathered by Margaret's munificence were among those to whom we owe all that we now know of Irish history; they were of the men who in the Irish revival of the thirteenth and fourteenth centuries spent their lives in searching out, preserving, copying, the records, laws, and traditions of their people. They were the lively translators of books from abroad, the students of the modern sciences, the band of scholars whose powerful influence was drawing the inhabitants of Ireland, English and Irish, into one culture. Their spirit is shewn in many sayings of the time.

"If you praise one for nobility praise his father likewise. If you praise one for his wealth, it is from the world it comes. If you praise one for his strength, know that sickness will render him weak, and if you praise a person for his fairness or the beauty of his body, know that the bloom of youth endures but a short while, and that age will take it away. But if you praise him for manners or learning, praise him as much as you will ever praise anyone, for this is the thing which comes not by heredity or through upbringing, but God bestowed it upon him as a gift."

"Wisdom is life and ignorance is death, for of God's gifts upon earth there is none which is higher and more comely and pure than wisdom, for to him who possesses it, wisdom teaches the performance of good things."

Such were the people whose culture had to be destroyed and their energies broken in the name of civilization. Twelve years later (1445) Margaret with a company of patriots—MacGeoghagans and others—hardened by long fighting, went on pilgrimage to St. James of Compostella, the shrine most dear to the Irish people, in the "fair Spain" whence their race had come. These pilgrimages are interesting, as showing the travel of Irishmen to Europe. In the *Cambridge Modern History* Ireland is described as "a mere *terra incognita*," cut off by its barbarism, and by its position from the larger influences of Europe: "of one Irish chieftain it was placed on record that he had accomplished the hazardous journey to Rome and back." In this half century alone (1396-1452) we read of two companies of chiefs and men of the poorer sort journeying to Compostella (1445, 1452), and of two companies who travelled to Rome (1396, 1444); and apparently of yet a third company, who brought back to Ireland tales they had heard of the French wars "from prisoners at Rome" (1451). By land and sea traders and scholars were crossing and re-crossing to the Continent, not only from one part of Ireland but from every province: "Do not repent," men said, "for going to acquire knowledge from a wise man, for merchants fare over the sea to add to their wealth."

Margaret returned to the distractions of a new conflict and the treacheries of a false peace (1445). Calvagh and the Berminghams were again making "a great war" with the English, cutting much corn and taking many prisoners, "and they made peace afterwards;" on which MacGeoghagan, just home from his pilgrimage, went with others under protection of the Baron of Delvin "where the English were"—that is to the Governor's castle at Trim. "But the English not regarding any peace took them all prisoners." MacGeoghagan was after that set at liberty, his son being given as hostage. "And Margaret, O'Carroll's daughter, went to Trim and gave all the English prisoners for MacGeoghagan's son and the son's son of Art, and that unadvised to Calvagh, and she brought them home." It was an act as free and brave as that of her daughter Finola, who had made peace for the O'Donnell land. Such women of great soul stand out on the stage of Irish history, nobly praised by the poets.

"She is sufficiently distinguished from every side
By her checking of plunder, her hatred of injustice,
By her serene countenance, which causes the trees
To bend with fruit; by her tranquil mind."

The story of Margaret was closing in sorrow. Finola, "the fairest and most famous woman in all Ireland beside her own mother," after the death of O'Donnell in the fifth year of his captivity in an English prison, married Aedh Boy O'Neill, "who was thought to be King of Ireland," "the most renowned, hospitable, and valourous of the princes in his time, and who had planted more of the lands of the English in despite of them than any other man of his day;" he was wounded to death on Spy-Wednesday (1444), "and we never heard since Christ was betrayed, on such a day a better man." A little later Finola, "renouncing all worldly vanity betook herself into the austere devout life in the monastery of Killeigh; and the blessing of guests and strangers, and poor and rich, of both poet-philosophers and archi-poet-philosophers be on her in that life" (1447). The next year Margaret's son, Cathal, was slain by the English of

Leinster. Calvagh, leading the Irish of Leinster in a great army, marched to Killculinn near the hill of Alenn on the border of the old Offaly, and there, his leg broken, his sword and helmet torn from him, the English horsemen were about to bring him into Castlemartin when "Cathal's son returned courageously and rescued him forceably." Another son Felim, heir to the lordship of Offaly, a man of great fame and renown, lay dying of long decline, on the night that Margaret herself passed away (1451). "A gracious year this year was, though the glory and solace of the Irish was set, but the glory of heaven was amplified and extolled therein." "The best woman of her time in Ireland"—such was the Irish record of that lofty and magnanimous soul. "God's blessing, the blessing of all saints, and every our blessing from Jerusalem to Inis Gluair be on her going to Heaven, and blessed be he that will read and hear this for blessing her soul."

Margaret left her husband to the gallant and hopeless struggle for the saving of Irish civilization. The next year he too made pilgrimage to Compostella (1452). But disaster gathered round him. MacGeoghagan, the most famous and renowned among the captains of Ireland, was slain, and his head carried to Trim and Dublin. Two sons of Calvagh were killed in war. His daughter Mòr, the wife of Clanricard, died of a fall from her horse; with her ended the system of alliances by which Calvagh had fortified himself west of the Shannon and in Ulster (1452). His old enemy Ormond, the best captain of the English in Ireland, he for whom the sun of old stood still, had come back to the Irish wars. He had been called to London in 1447 on a charge of treason, for trial by battle with his chief foe the Prior of Kilmainham—Ormond by the King's leave staying at Smithfield "for his breathing and more ease" while he trained for the fight; the Prior learning "certain points of arms" from a fishmonger paid by the King. But the royal favour prevailed, Ormond made clear his desire to exterminate the Irish, and without trial or battle was declared "whole and untainted in fame." He returned to ravage Kildare and Meath in war with the rival house of the FitzGeralds, earls of Kildare, and to make a last triumphant march round the bordering Irish tribes. Calvagh was forced to "come into his house" and make terms of peace (1452). The peace was made null by Ormond's death a month later, and Calvagh "went out into the wilderness of Kildare" where the new deputy with his cavalry surrounded him unawares. Teige, his son, "most courageously worked to rescue his father from the English horsemen; but O'Connor's horse fell thrice down to the ground, and Teige put him up twice, and O'Connor himself would not give his consent the third time to go with him, so that then O'Connor was taken prisoner." The same year he was released. But his wars were practically over. In 1458 he was buried by his father Murchadh and his wife Margaret in Killeigh; defender of his country for sixty years, and for thirty-seven years lord of Offaly. Last of all, Finola, after forty-six years of the religious life (1493), rested also in the splendid abbey of Killeigh.

Of the glories of that abbey, of its rich glass, its gold and silver work, its sculptured tombs, its organs, nothing now remains but a bare fragment of wall. In the year that Silken Thomas and his five uncles were hanged at Tyburn (1537), Lord Leonard Grey wasted the land of O'Connor Faly, who had married the sister of Earl Thomas; making him "more like a beggar, than he that ever was a captain or ruler of a country." Vast quantities of corn stored up at Killeigh were carried to the Pale; and from the ruined Abbey Grey furnished out the buildings of Maynooth, which had been stormed and taken from Earl Thomas two years before; carrying off from its sack a pair of organs and other necessary things for the King's College at Maynooth, and as much glass as was needed to glaze the windows of the College and of His Grace's Castle there. The tombs of the great house of O'Connor Faly were utterly destroyed so that no trace of them remains.

The destruction of the great abbey was the symbol to the Leinster Irish of their final desolation, the ruin which submerged the whole people of Ireland on the fall of the House of Kildare. Then began in the rich plains of Leinster the ruthless policy of wholesale extirpation of the Irish old inhabitants, to "plant" the country anew from across the sea. The fruitful land became to Irish eyes a vast cemetery of their dead. In their lamentation they remembered that Brian Boru's grave was there, and the grave of his son "that bore the brunt of weapon-fight": and still the graves were multiplied. "Great are the charges that all others have against the land of Leinster"—a poet of the O'Byrnes sang.... "Charges against her all Ireland's nobles have: that beneath the salmon-abounding Leinster country's soil—region of shallow rivers foamy-waved—there is many a grave of their kings and of their heirs apparent." "The red-handed Leinster province" holds the bones of the long line of O'Connor Faly, men and women who adorned their country with courage and piety, art and learning.

"They shall be remembered for ever,
They shall be speaking for ever,
The people shall hear them for ever."

CHAPTER IV

A CASTLE AT ARDGLASS.

THE "island of Lecale," as the Elizabethan English called it, lies in the County of Down, surrounded on three sides by the sea, and on the fourth bounded by the Quoile and Blackstaff rivers. The northern coast of the "island" almost closes the mouth of Lough Cuan, now Strangford Lough, leaving but a narrow strait for boats to pass. On the south it bounds the Bay of Dundrum, across which rises the huge granite mass of the Mourne Mountains.

The fruitful plain of Lecale, defended and enriched by the sea, drew to it inhabitants from the first peopling of Ireland. All Irish history is reflected there. The in-comers of prehistoric times raised the great stone circles of Ballyno, that stupendous monument to a great hero and a solemn worship—none more astonishing in Ireland. On a wide slope, completely shut off and secluded by the higher ground, the rings of massive stones lie confronting alone the eminence on which is lifted up against the heavens the imposing mound of Erenagh, loftiest of the line of earthworks that surround Dundrum Bay. From the time of an immemorial Nature worship pilgrims have assembled, even as they gathered down to our own times, where the streams of Struel pour abundantly from the rock, to seek cleansing in the bounteous waters on Midsummer Day, and at the festival of Lughnasadh or Lugh's fair on the first of August. The Red Branch of Emain sent its heroes to hold the two main passages into the "island," and the inlets of the sea where trade was borne. On the northern port, known to Ptolemy as Dunum, where the river Quoile widens to Strangford Lough, Celtchair of the Battles made his entrenchment of Rath Celtchair or Dun Lethglasse, on a hill rising from the flat ground and swamps of the river. At the head of Dundrum Bay, where the sea narrows over a stretch of shoals and shallows to the inner bay, another Red Branch knight raised on a steep rock his commanding fort, Dún Rudraidhe, and left his name also to the ocean tide, Tonn Rudraidhe, whose waters were lifted up into one of the Three Waves of Ireland that sounded their warning to the land when danger threatened, or echoed the moan in battle of a dying hero's shield. Here, in this place of Celtic legend, relics of bronze and pottery and stone can still be picked up in plenty on the sand dunes. Round the circuit of the bay half-a-dozen ancient earthworks may still be seen, connected with strands or harbours by old paths.

With the dawn of a new age the wanderings of St. Patrick gave to Lecale new memories—the wells which he blessed for the new faith; the wooden barn at Saul where he set up his church on the slope above the marsh along which the highway ran from Strangford to Down, and where the angel called him to die; the Dun of Patrick, or Downpatrick, given him for a Christian settlement on the old rath of Celtchair, where according to later legend he was buried, and where a great granite boulder now marks the traditional grave. Amid the majestic monuments of pagan heroes the lowly pioneers of the new faith raised their little buildings. The spit of land that separates the bay of Tonn Rudraidhe from that of Ardglass is fringed with low rocks black and jagged; and this point of danger to mariners, now marked by a lighthouse, was in early Christian times sanctified by a church. A tiny harbour cuts through the keen-edged rocks to a little strand where a couple of curraghs might lie: and there by the well the little company built their church—a small stone building twenty feet by thirteen, with the two narrow windows, one east and one south, to throw on the altar the light of the rising and the midday sun, and the western door for the departing day and the hour of benediction till the sun should make his circuit to the east. The name of St. John's Point recalls that old dedication, and the early Irish devotion to their special saint, the beloved disciple of the Lord. Across the bay might be seen the austere cell of St. Donard lifted high, near 3,000 feet, on the topmost point of Slieve-Donard, dominating all Lecale, where an inspired solitary transformed the ancient pagan tradition to a new use, that as mighty men of old were in death commemorated by carns on the high hills, so on the mountain a Christian would shew afar the place of his burial to the world, and the place of his resurrection.

Lecale was soon filled with religious settlements and schools. Lying at the entrance to Lough Cuan of the hundred islands, now Lough Strangford, where a busy population tilled the fertile slopes, and sent out innumerable boats for the celebrated salmon-fishing, or for traffic, Lecale was as it were the guardian of their sanctuaries. Close to Downpatrick lies Crannach Dún-leth-glaisse, "the wooded island of Dún-leth-glaisse," now known as Cranny island; there Mochuaróc maccu Min Semon, whom the Romans called the "doctor" of the whole world, lived early in the seventh century, and wrote down the calculus which his master Sinlan, Abbot of Bangor (+610), had first among the Irish learned from a certain wise Greek. Farther north, some twelve or fifteen miles from Ardglass, lies Inis-Mahee, where behind the boulder-strewn shore and the heavy seaweed thrown up by the waters on meadows and ploughed land over which sea-birds love to hover, past the harbour and the rude boat-shelter cut in the rock, we enter on a retreat where the light seems more translucent than elsewhere, the silence more penetrating and peace more profound, the colour as that of an everlastingspring—a space of wild wood, resonant with the song of birds, where the flowers spring thicker than the grass. There St. Mochaoi (Mahee) raised his wooden church about 450 A.D., first abbot and bishop. Legend told that as he was cutting wattles for his building, he heard a bright bird, more beautiful than the birds of the world, singing on the blackthorn near him, and asked who it was that made such a song. "A man of the people of my Lord," answered the bird. "Hail," said Mochaoi, "and for why that, oh bird that is an angel?" "I am come by command to encourage you in your good work, and because of the love that is in your heart to amuse you for a time with my sweet singing." "I am glad of that," said Mochaoi. One hundred and fifty years passed as a moment while he listened to the heavenly song; and when the bird vanished and he lifted up his bundle of wattles to carry home, a stone church stood there before him, and strange monks. They made him abbot once more; and there at last "a sleep without decay of the body Mochaoi slept." The foundations of the little church with walls over three feet thick, the remnant of the round tower, the traces of other buildings on the west of the island hill, the well closed in, the triple ring of earthen entrenchments faced with stone that encircled the slopes of the island like a cashel, the port with its rough stone work into which "ships from Britain" sailed—these still tell of the days when Inis-Mahee was a school of religion and learning for all the district, where the famous St. Finian of Moville came to study. From the round tower the whole lough could be seen as far as Lecale and the passage to the sea. There must have been then, as there was later, much intercourse between the sea-going people of Mahee and Ardglass. For Ardglass was the port of the neighbouring monastery whose site we may still trace at Dunsford. A Protestant church was planted over it in Reformation times; but an old cross slab may still be seen, and from the graveyard there has been rescued an ancient stone font, and carried to the new church of the older faith; and here too an ancient Celtic cross from an old cemetery, of the type of those found at Clonmacnois, has been set over the church door.

Lecale was a rich land to plunder when the Danes descended on it. Not a creek that they did not visit. Their raids were followed by later raids of their Norman kinsmen, when in 1177 de Courcy came marching to the conquest of Ulster, dreaming himself the knight foretold by Merlin, and willing "to accommodate himself in dress, in gesture, in his shield, and even his white horse, to the prophecies; so that he looked more like a Merry-Andrew than a warrior." The seizing of Lecale and Downpatrick was his first adventure; before a year was over (1178) he had attached Mahee to an English monastery, peopled it with monks from the other side of the sea, and along with Roger, the new lord of Dunsford, endowed it with large tracts of land about Dunsford and in Lecale. In spite of new wealth the spirit and fortunes of Mahee died for ever under foreign rule.

By de Courcy and his followers the island of Lecale was ringed with castles from the great keep of Dundrum ("it is one of the strongest holds I ever saw," said Lord Leonard Grey) to Downpatrick at the passage of the Quoile. The memory of one of his Norman knights is preserved in Dunsford church, a grave-slab with a fine cross and sword cut deeply on it, perhaps the tombstone of "Rogerus de Dunsford." The strong rush of waters that poured through the narrow neck of Lough Cuan at every incoming or outgoing tide, once guarded on either side by earthen entrenchments that may still be seen, was now held by a Norman keep at Strangford; but the towers of the coast line from Ardglass to Down—Kilclief, Walsh's castle, Audley castle, Quoile castle, and the rest—each set at the head of a little bay, were evidently planted there for trade; and all probably on the sites of older Irish communities. Thus at Kilclief, while Norman cross slabs tell of de Courcy's plantation, there is in the churchyard a long forgotten tombstone marked with a Celtic cross of the type of Clonmacnois. How many were thrown out to build fences, or to be broken on the roads! The activity of trade along the coast even as late as the eighteenth century may be seen by the remains at Quoile harbour near Down, the custom-house, the great stores, the houses of merchants and officials of the harbour.

In the 106 miles of coast that lie between Kingstown mole and Belfast bay, Ardglass is the one harbour where a ship can enter at all stages of the tide without a local pilot. It must ever have been a chief harbour of eastern Ulster—a port open at all times of the tide and sheltered from every wind save one, when boats could take refuge in the southern port of Killough, "the haven of Ardglass," linked with it by an old path along the shore. A wall was thrown round the little town of Ardglass strengthened by seven towers, four of which may still be seen; and within these defences a central castle was set on the rocky edge of the port, where boats could be pulled up to the very door. The harbour was the outlet for the trade of the rich agricultural and wool-producing lands of Down, Tyrone, and Armagh, and traffic was carried on in wines, cloth, kerseys, all kinds of fish, wool, and tallow. There is evidence of trade with France in the beautiful altar-vessel found at Bright, of gilt bronze and many shaded enamel, fine Limoges work of about 1200 A.D.

With the revival of Irish life in the fourteenth century, and the gatherings of English merchants to Irish fairs, commerce increased and flourished. Richard II. gave the port of Ardglass and its trade as a rich reward to the Gascon commander, Janico d'Artois, his bravest leader against Art MacMurchadh (1398). It is said that a trading company with a grant from Henry IV. built the famous "New Works." Close to the harbour ran a range of buildings two hundred and fifty feet long, with three square towers, walls three feet thick, pierced on the sea-side by only narrow loop-holes, and opening into the "bawn" with sixteen square windows, and fifteen arched door-ways of cut stone that gave entrance to eighteen rooms on the ground floor and eighteen above. It is still possible to trace the line of the New Works, the doors and windows, and the remains of the towers. There seems to have been a local school of art continued from the earlier centuries: fragments of a Virgin and Child of old Dunsford made by Irish hands of Irish stone from Scrabo at the north end of Strangford Lough, broken and scattered for ages, have been recovered and pieced together and set on the wall of the new Dunsford church, where it now stands in its old grace and dignity as the only example in Ulster, perhaps in Ireland, of such a pre-Reformation statue not utterly destroyed. All the churches of Lecale, old men told a traveller about 1643, had before the burnings of Captain Edward Cromwell been lightly roofed, probably with fine open wood-carving, and highly adorned with sacred statues and images.

From a few fragments we can only guess what wealth was once stored up in Lecale. Wars of Irish and English raged round a harbour so important, as the chiefs of Ulster pressed down against the strangers over a land which had once at Dun Lethglasse held a chief fort of old Ulster kings. O'Neill burned Ardglass of the d'Artois house in 1433: in 1453 Henry O'Neill of Clannaboy was driven back from the town by the help of a Dublin fleet. At the close of the fifteenth century the English almost disappeared out of Lecale. Garrett the Great, Earl of Kildare (1477-1513), claimed Ardglass and the lands about it as heir through his mother to d'Artois, and gained supremacy there—a part of the far-seeing policy by which the house of Kildare was gradually widening its influence from sea to sea, from Ardglass to Sligo and the lower Shannon. His son Garrett Oge had, by grant of Henry VIII. (1514), the customs of

Strangford and Ardglass, to be held by service of one red rose annually; and still after four centuries heirs of the Fitzgerald house remain at the entrance of Strangford Lough. After the revolt of this Garrett's son, Silken Thomas (1535), the English marched through the country, burning Lecale. The fall of the Kildares, allies and relatives of the O'Neills, brought a revival of the O'Neill wars for Ardglass, and of the English campaigns. Lord Leonard Grey has left a description in the State Papers (III. 155) of his expedition in 1539: "and so with the host we set forward into the said country and took all the castles there and delivered them to Mr. Treasurer who hath warded the same ... the said Lecayll is environed round about with the sea and no way to go by land into said country but only by the castle of Dundrome.... I assure your lordship I have been in many places and countries in my days and yet did I never see for so much a pleasanter plot of ground than the said Lecayll, for the commodity of the land and divers islands in the same environed with the sea which were soon reclaimed and inhabited...."

It was in this "reclaiming" that the Deputy ravaged the east coast, took Dundrum, and the castles of Lecale and Ards; profaned S. Patrick's Church at Down, turning it into a stable and destroying the monuments of Patrick, Brigid, and Columcille, and "after plucked it down, and shipped the notable ring of bells that did hang in the steeple, meaning to have them sent to England: had not God of his justice prevented his iniquity by sinking the vessel and passengers." Queen Mary restored Ardglass to the next Earl, Gerald, son of Silken Thomas, the boy who at his father's capture had escaped "tenderly wrapped" in a turf-basket, and after long perils and sorrows and exile in Rome, Italy, and France, had at last returned, an obedient Angliciser under the Catholic queen (1553). Under Queen Elizabeth, who was in Irish belief illegitimate and a usurper, Shane O'Neill (1558-1567) cast out the English, and "forcibly patronised himself in all Lecale." Ardglass seems to have come into the hands of the Irish, and trade was busy, for in Shane's great cellars at Dundrum he was said to have commonly stored two hundred tuns of wine.

Thirty years after Shane's death (1597), a plan for out-rooting the Irish and planting an English race was drawn up by a clergyman of "the

Church of Ireland," James Bell, Vicar of Christ Church in Dublin, and dedicated by him to Lord Burghley. He was the faithful representative of a political establishment, deep-stained with the blood and sorrow of the Irish. Here is his proposal, preserved in the British Museum: "The Crown should divide the land into lots of 300 acres, at £5 yearly rent, for *English* undertakers, who should maintain 10 men (English) and 10 women, who now live in England by begging and naughty shifts; while single to have two acres, married, four acres of the 300—which was to be circumvallated by a deep trench or fosse.... If upon Tirone's lands 2,000 English families be planted, her Majesty's profit would at once be £10,000; besides, having 4,000 soldiers at hand without pay, for every two of the ten men should serve in turn three months each year—the act would be *motherly* and honourable for her Highness. To the bishops, there should be given, in fee simple, 1,200 acres, at £20 a year, upon every 300 acres of which the ten men and women are to be maintained, upon the like conditions; the inferior clergy, down to parson and curate, to have 600 acres upon proportionate rent and service. If her Majesty's heart be moved by this device, there shall not be a beggar in England; a work of great profit, great strength, and great glory to the Queen, great love to her subjects, and singular mercy towards her meanest subjects, in that she giveth house and lands in Ireland to those that, in England, have not a hole to hide their heads in. The trench round about would barr Irish rebels coming suddenly trotting and jumping upon the good English subjects." In the proposed commonwealth no room for sustenance was left for the Irish people of the land, fenced off from every place of food. Loyal to her Majesty, James Bell was yet more loyal to the material predominance of his Church. Among farmers owning three hundred acres with ten families of labourers, the Church of Ireland was to have a stately position with its inferior curates owning twice as much as their best neighbours, and the bishops four times as much. It was but an act of gratitude. "I will not say as Joshua and Caleb said, if the Lord have a favour unto us; but I will say, the Lord having a special love unto us, God hath given Ireland to her Majesty—a country most sweet, most wholesome, and most fruitful to dwell in; so full of springs, so full of rivers, so full of lakes, so full of fish, so full of cattle, and of fowl, that there is not a country upon the face of the earth more beneficial to the life of man."

Thus plans of settlement and plantation were abroad when Mountjoy led his army over Lecale. The castle of Dundrum surrendered to him (1601). "His Lordship ... rode to Downpatrick, and thence by St. Patrick's Well to Ardglass, being six miles, in which town two castles yielded to the Queen, and the warders, upon their lives saved, gave up their arms. A third castle there had been held for the Queen all the time of the Rebellion, by one Jordan, never coming out of the same for three years past, till now by his Lordship's coming he was freed." This was the castle on the port, which was evidently provisioned from the sea, the only stronghold left in Ardglass for the English, and called Castle Jordan from its defender. After this subjection of Ardglass, Sir Richard Morrison, with five hundred foot and fifty horse, was left at Downpatrick as governor of Lecale, while Mountjoy carried on war against Tyrone.

A picture of life in a Lecale castle at this time has been left to us by Captain Josias Bodley, of Mountjoy's army. From Armagh to Newry he journeyed through a famished country where for a whole year Chichester's and Morrison's troops had been employed in completely devastating the land, so that O'Neill should get provision neither for man nor horse; and the poverty he saw in Newry shows their success. Thence skirting the Mourne Mountains he stopped at the island stronghold of Magennis in the lake at Castlewellan, and passing through a land of ancient cromlechs and souterrains, of earthworks ringed and conical, and of early Norman castles, entered Lecale. The scene of the final merry-makings, the Governor's Castle at Downpatrick, was probably the fort which stood at the foot of the hill, the last remains of which, a tall square tower, were removed a few years ago. It was evidently not unlike the castle at Ardglass, and life was the same in both of them. The stairs led first to the guard-room, with its dresser laden with dishes, and a wide fire-place where heavy pots hung from iron crooks, and cooks were busy with interminable cooking of the fish and fowls and game for which Lecale was famous, pasties of marrow and plums, Irish curds, and other dishes from France, there designated "Quelq' choses" ("kickshaws"), which were reckoned "vulgar" by the English officers, as being perhaps too little substantial. Thence the stairs led to the large hall where in the huge fire-place logs were burning, even as in Castle Shane of Ardglass to-day, "the height of our chins, as the saying is." The hall was comfortable, for of a night one may sit in the Ardglass room with the unglazed windows in the thick walls on every side, and the door open to the winding stairs, and no flicker of candles betrays a draught: the wind seems carried up the turret staircase through the roof. The company in the hall amused themselves with smoking, cards, backgammon, and dice. There was much drinking of healths—many political pledges no doubt as in modern Ulster, bitter tests to Irish companions when the English officers might call on a newly-submitted chief such as Magennis to join in a "loyal" toast: Bodley had apparently taken part in some scenes of scruple and silence on the part of honourable men, "of all things the most shameful," he says. For any special entertainment the servants crowded into the same room as the masters—the cook's wife, the scullion, and all; and played to amuse them a game still common in the north. There came, too, the Irish Mummers or Rhymers, making their Christmas rounds with torches and drums, wearing the traditional pointed caps, and carrying their profits in the base money, one part of silver to three of brass, which Elizabeth forced upon Ireland in favour of her avaricious Treasurer there, Sir George Carey. Of this money, such as it was, the Rhymers were "cleaned out" by the officers in a game of dice, and sent on their long walk home across Lecale two hours after the winter midnight, "without money; out of spirits; out of order; without even saying 'Farewell'"—a strange contrast to the old Irish welcome to travellers and wandering players—a gallant hospitality at the Christmas time of English officers, for whom no season of mercy was sacred, and no obligation of honour, straight dealing, or courtesy binding so far as Irishmen were concerned. The rhymers may have sung as they took their way the fame of the hero-warrior of their people: "Were but the brown leaf which the wood sheds from it gold, were but the white billows silver, Finn would have given it all away." They may have recalled the lament of the old Irish poet who saw the havoc made by "outlanders" of the ordered hospitality of Irish society. "At the end of the final world [there will be] a refuge to poverty and stinginess and grudging." They could not see in the far future the open castle of Ardglass.

Cards, dice, drinking, and smoking filled up the time of the English visitors, with strolls of curiosity to the Wells and Chair of St. Patrick at Struel, or the huge entrenchments of Celtchair of the Battles. For the night there was a single sleeping-room above the hall, a bed-chamber "arranged in the Irish fashion" with a good and soft bed of down for the owner, and thin pallets thrown on the floor for the company. The dogs of Captain Constable shared the room with the rest, after the Yorkshire manner, leaping on the down bed and howling at their rejection.

When Morrison left Downpatrick there came Captain Edward Cromwell —descendant of Thomas Cromwell, minister of ill-fame to Ireland under Henry VIII.—to be Governor of Lecale (1605): "this son of earth and foul spot on the human race," by whose army the cathedral of Down was burned, and in that conflagration sacred monuments and very ancient writings; and many other churches too, very few of which have been since then restored. The very tombstones were used in building houses and fences; while the people watching lamented the devastation of what had been to them and their fathers "the place of their resurrection," so that they might go in the fellowship of their saints "to the great assembly of Doom." To Edward Cromwell the people gave the name "Maol-na-teampull" for his impiety, and numbers of men born in that terrible year of ruin reckoned their age over sixty years after from the days of his sacrilege, as if from a national visitation. In those days perhaps the Irish inhabitants were driven off the fertile land to the very rim of the sea, to set their cabins, as may still be seen, on the last refuge of the shingle itself round the Dundrum bay, or to cluster together on some bare crag.

After the wars of Mountjoy and of Cromwell and the plantations of their officers the fortunes of Lecale, as of all Ireland, declined. With the final ruin of the O'Neills the clouded title of the Fitzgeralds revived, in a dim shadow of their old pride. A branch of the family built, in the eighteenth century, a sober mansion over the "New Works" that had been raised when Ireland claimed her right to trade, and around the towers that marked ancient centuries of battle. Even there the old Fitzgerald fires of patriotism and indignation at inhuman wrong broke out anew. The character of Lord Edward Fitzgerald is as little comprehended as the spirit of his country. A Protestant brought up in the days of penal laws and Protestant ascendancy; a member of the great house of the Duke of Leinster in Ireland and the Duke of Richmond in England; trained in an army fighting for "the Empire" against American "rebels"; his life till twenty-seven was chiefly spent in France, America, and England, amid military and aristocratic society—conditions that have made many a man cosmopolitan, denationalised, and indifferent. The liberal traditions of his father, the first Duke of Leinster, had practically died with him when the boy was only ten. Ardently devoted to his family, there was not one of them, or one of his early friends, to whom he could speak of his national beliefs. And out of all this came the lover of the poor and the oppressed, the friend of all men, the intrepid martyr to the freedom of Catholic Ireland, dying alone in prison with a prayer for the salvation of all who died at the hangman's hands for the sake of Ireland. No wonder that the people of Ardglass still show the tower chamber in the old castle which was searched for Lord Edward, the room in the great house where he was said to have hidden, the rude bridge that gave him shelter from the yeomanry, and the desolate site of Bone castle where he slept for one night, in an ancient possession of his family.

In the course of the gloomy years that followed the old house fell into decay. Last June (1911) the whole derelict property, long deserted by its landlords, both land and village, was sold for the benefit of English mortgagees and bought by local people. Nothing more "loyal" could be imagined than the apparent community of Ardglass—nothing more to the heart of the party in Down and Antrim of superiority and supremacy which claims sole right to a place in the sun. The Imperial flag flew from a high-lifted residence, on the site of two of the old forts. The FitzGerald house and demesne were bought by a golf club, reputed to be faithful above all to English interests. The old castle was bid for by a spirit-dealer of the right persuasion, as a suitable storage place for whiskey. Not a breath as to the destiny of Ardglass and its fishermen disturbed the peace of Orangemen and stalwart Protestants of the ascendancy.

It occurred, however, to a good Irishman and antiquary, a Protestant from Belfast, that there might be a nobler use for the Castle of Ardglass. He bought the castle. He replaced the vanished floors and ceilings with beams and boards of Irish timber. A few broken pieces of masonry were repaired. The inside walls were left in their rough state, merely dashed with white. At the door was laid the anvil of an Irish smith to be held between the knees, a stone with the centre cut out and fitted with iron. The great fire-places were filled with logs from a local plantation. Over the flaming fires huge pots steamed, hanging from iron crooks. Old Ulster ironwork for kitchen use hung round the hearth. A dresser, such as Captain Bodley might have seen, was stocked with pewter plates and old crockery, brought, like the ironwork, by willing givers who possessed any relic of Ireland of former days. Tables of Irish oak, and Irish carved benches of the old fashion, and Irish cupboards and settles furnished the rooms. They were lighted by Irish-made candles in the iron taper-holders of over a hundred years ago, by a very remarkable bronze chandelier of the eighteenth century, and by a still more striking floreated cross and circle of lights, made in the penal days by some local metal-worker with the ancient Irish tradition of ornament still with him. In the chief room a few old prints and portraits hung on the walls, amid new banners representing O'Neill, O'Donnell, and the black Raven of the Danes; most prominent of all, Shane O'Neill himself, standing proud in his full height in regal saffron kilt and flowing mantle, a fine design by a young Irish artist of Belfast. A tiny round-apsed oratory opened off this chief room. It was hung with golden Irish linen; between the lights on the altar stood a small crucifix of the penal times, and interlaced Irish patterns hung on the walls. The columbary in one of the towers, perhaps unique in early castles, with its seventy-five triangular recesses or resting-places for the pigeons built in the walls, and entries to north and south—one a square opening with sill inside and alighting slab outside, the other a space cut below the narrow window exactly the size through which a bird might pass—was again stocked with pigeons given by a local admirer, and the tower named after St. Columba. From a pole flew the flag of O'Neill, the Red Right Hand, in memory of old days. In three months the deserted ruin was transformed into a dwellinghouse, where Mr. Bigger and his helpers could sleep and cook and live. The workmen in a fury of enthusiasm worked as if a master's eye was on them at every minute.

The design of the new owner was to bring the people of Ardglass and the Lecale of Down into touch with the Irish past, and give them some conception of the historic background of their life. For it must be remembered that through all conquests and plantations the people of the soil of Lecale have still remained of the old stock, an Irish people who have a natural country to love. For them there need be none of the perplexities which must confront those who in their successive generations of life in Ireland still consent to be designated by *The Times* as "the British Colony on the other side of St. George's Channel." I was present on the Saturday night when the ruin was opened to the people. There was no moon, and a gale was blowing down the Irish Sea —a wind from the north. A little platform was set against the sheltered west wall of the castle. A beacon flamed on one of the towers, and the ceremony began with a display of limelight pictures on the wall. I was in the middle of an audience packed as tight as men could stand in the castle yard and across the wide street. There had been no public announcements and no advertisement. But word had passed round the people of Lecale, and it seemed as if thousands had gathered under the resplendent stars. "I do not mean to show you," said Mr. Bigger, "China or Japan; I mean to show you Ardglass." The audience went wild with delight to see their fishermen and women, their local celebrities, the boats laden with fish, the piles on the pier, the Donegal girls packing them, the barrels rolled out to the tramp steamers. But the delight reached its utmost height at views of the sea taken from a boat out fishing, the dawn of day, the early flight of birds, the swell of the great waters. The appeal of beauty brought a rich answer from the Irish crowd.

Then there was Irish dancing and singing on the little platform, with the grey wall of the castle as a background and the waving ivy branches and tree shadows in the limelight, a scene of marvellous light and shade. But the great moment of all came when a huge Irish flag was flung out on the night wind from the Columba tower. I have never seen so magic a sight. Lights blazed from the castle-roof, rockets flamed across the sky, and in the midst suddenly appeared like a vision among the host of stars (for no flag-staff could be seen against the night-sky) a gleaming golden harp hanging secure in immensity, crossed and re-crossed by balls and flames of fire, so that it seemed to escape only by a miracle.

How did Ardglass and Lecale take this revival of its older fame? That sight was not less striking than the vision on the tower. Every cottage in the village had candles set in its windows. The fisher-boats in the harbour were alight; they flew flags too, and Irish flags, as many as could get them. For hours crowds climbed and descended the narrow winding staircase in the castle turret, lighted by candles fixed in old Ulster iron holders. They thronged the rooms, themselves the guardians of all the treasures lying on the benches and shelves and suspended on the walls. When they drew aside the light curtain before the oratory and entered in, they prostrated themselves, kneeling in prayer, and came out with tears in their eyes. Young men looked at Shane O'Neill, and looked again, and took off their hats. As in other Irish gatherings where I have been, sobriety and good manners distinguished the crowd, very visible and audible to me from my little hotel fronting the castle where the visitors flocked for refreshment, under my window opening on the one street of the village. Strangers dispersed about eleven o'clock, but men of the village sat round the fire of the old guard-room for hours after, singing songs of Ireland endlessly. There was no host, and no master of the ceremonies. The castle was left absolutely to the people. Anyone who would came in. They sang, and sang, the sorrowful decadent songs of modern Ireland—songs of famine, emigration, lamentation, and woe. But still they sang of Ireland.

The next day was Sunday. The parish priest, many years among his people, shared in the joy of the festival, in the new interest come to break the long monotony of their life, and in the widening and lifting of their emotion. He preached twice on the restoration to them of their castle, and on their duty to hold it sacred, and to act with courtesy and good breeding when they entered it. He gave the children freedom from Sunday School that they might see the Irish flag flown from the tower at noon; and boys and girls poured laughing down the street. All that day, from morning till night, without a pause, lines of village and country folk filed up and down the turret stairs, holding to the rope, kept taut by its old stone weight, that served as balustrade. Protestants were intermingled with Catholics, as one could see by the badges of their societies, in a common enthusiasm for the memories of the country which was theirs. Two admirable little girls of nine and fourteen installed themselves as handmaids and hostesses of the castle, and might be seen all day carrying water to the cauldron, making tea, giving hospitality to visitors—their first free service to Ireland. At night, men and women of the village came into the guard-room and banquet-hall, and sang and sang of Ireland. They did not even smoke. One after another sang till one o'clock. One or two sentimental ditties turned up, on Shannon's shores and Killarney's lakes, of the feeble artificial sort favoured by so-called "National Schools," but these found little encouragement. Many evenings since, the guard-room has been filled with villagers, and singing and old-time lore abound. Many bring presents and leave them with scarce a word; and the old oratory has not been left without gifts and flowers. Nowhere has a pin been disturbed, or a trifle broken or injured. The battlements and the glorious view are a delight to all. They examine and point out to each other the old devices, the flint weapons and the bronze, the Celtic emblems and memorials, and the Elizabethan and Volunteer arms that lie about. The people have a new pride put in them, and are learning to be their own Conservators and Board of Works.

The Bishop of Ossory has lately given us all to understand that the Church of Ireland, boasting itself to be the highest, perhaps the sole, regenerating force in the country, is at this crisis altogether absorbed in anxious contemplation of the supposed danger from the people of Ireland to its property. A material preoccupation, at such a pitch, induces a multitude of unreasoning timidities, fantastic safeguards, and voluntary solitudes. It is true, indeed, that it was only "property" in a spiritual sense which the people of Ardglass had got that day. But in that higher sense they had been given that which every Irishman lacks—something of their own. No Englishman can picture to himself that lack. He has never had it. But with us it is an old story. If the people ask to learn Irish—"Here is arithmetic; that will suit you better." They would like something of Irish history—"I assure you that it is German grammar which you really wish to ask for." If the talk is of schools or fisheries—"The English Treasury will see that you do not waste money on school-house or steam trawler." Their very names are not their own. A Belfast bank the other day refused the life-long signature on a cheque of a well-known Irish writer because he signed, in English letters indeed, but with his customary Irish spelling of Padraic, and required instead the conventional English Patrick. Who can tell the needless restrictions and trivialities and imposed fashions that check expansion, experiment, and freedom of mind? A dreary emptiness has been stretched over the vivid natures of Irishmen. What is there left for them to love? Is it any wonder they desire something they may call their own? It may be that "Loyalists" imagine that a longer continuance of such destitution will end at last in a lively passion for Englishmen and the Empire. Or, perhaps, it is the Unionist idea that an enforced apathy indefinitely continued will produce the fate that comes on men doomed to imprisonment for life in solitary confinement, when after long years thought and speech are gone, and idiot prisoners may mingle harmlessly together.

While the castle was repairing at Ardglass, an Irish visitor watched the fishermen leaning on the sea-wall. Every half-hour one might drop a word. They were passing the time as only fishermen know how. As to the castle, they looked as oblivious to it as to everything else. After watching for some time, the Irish visitor casually passed one of them, dropping an indifferent remark: "What's the meaning of all this?" "It's comin'," said the fisherman. "We're too long held in chains"—and fell back into silence.

NOTE.

Bodley's visit to Lecale, preserved in a Latin MSS. in the British Museum, has been printed with a translation in the Old Ulster Journal of Archæology II. 73. The account is concerned with six officers of high rank and fame in the veteran army of Elizabeth. The writer, Captain Bodley, brother of the founder of the Bodleian Library at Oxford, was commanding officer at Armagh, commissioned to raise fortifications or entrenchments for the army—"a very honest fellow with a black beard," he describes himself. His companion Captain Toby Caulfield, who had fought at Carlingford and Kinsale, was the first Governor in 1602 of the new fort of Charlemont, and Governor in 1603 of the counties of Armagh and Tyrone, where he made good use of his opportunities, a skilful appropriator of lands, who secured for himself grants in nine counties, and the wealth on which the earldom of Charlemont was established. Captain John Jephson had rescued the remnant of the British army caught in the pass of the Curlew Mountains in 1599: he gained the Mallow estate by marriage with the daughter of Norreys, President of Munster. Captain Adderton, whom they picked up on the way, had distinguished himself in the Wicklow wars, and was now Governor of the newly-built fort of Mount-norris, on the road from Armagh to Newry.

Their host at Downpatrick, Sir Richard Moryson, one of the chief friends of Mountjoy, had fought in Leix and at Kinsale, was now Governor of Lecale, and this same year (1603) was promoted Governor of Waterford, and later (1607), President of Munster. With him was Captain Ralph Constable, who had followed all his campaigns from Kinsale to the Blackwater.

Four of the six, Moryson, Bodley, Jephson, and Caulfield, had been comrades in the campaigns of the Low Countries a few years before, and were among the companies of soldiers which were drafted over from the Netherlands to Ireland to strengthen the armies of Essex and Mountjoy. They were men who prospered in Irish wars—keen soldiers, and as keen dividers of lands and offices in the new country, deeply concerned in plantations and confiscations.

An Account of a Journey of Captain Josias Bodley into Lecale in Ulster, in the Year 1602 (properly 1603).

Good God! what have I taken on me to do? Truly I am an ass, otherwise I would never have undertaken so heavy a burthen; but no matter, I shall do what I can, like Coppinger's female dog, who always took her own way.

I have taken in hand to recount what happened in a journey which Captain Caulfield, Captain Jephson, and I made to Lecale, to visit our friend Sir Richard Morrison, and divert ourselves there. And I shall narrate everything in due order; for order is a fair thing, and all love it, except the Irish men-at-arms, who are a most vile race of men, if it be at all allowable to call them "men," who live upon grass, and are foxes in their disposition and wolves in their actions. But to our business: The aforesaid Master Morrison sent very kind letters to us, inviting us to keep the Nativity (which the English call "Christmas") with him; but as Sir

Arthur Chichester, the Sergeant-Major of the whole army, had convoked us with all our companies at that very moment to fight with Tyrone, who was then in the woods of Glenconkein with much cattle and few fighting men; we could not go at that time to Lecale, but joined the said Sir Arthur, and remained with him for sixteen or seventeen days in the field, without doing much harm to Tyrone: for that Tyrone is the worst rascal, and very wary and subtle, and won't be beaten except on good terms. However, we fought him twice in the very woods, and made him run to his strongholds. So after leaving about that place a well-provided garrison, we each departed, with full permission and good will.

We now remembered the said invitation of Sir Richard and, after deliberation (for, in the commencement of affairs, deliberation should be used by those adventuring bold attempts, as Seneca says), we thought it good to go thither, although it was now eight days after the Nativity: because we did not doubt our being welcome though it had been Lent. This was resolved on in the city of Armagh, where there is a Governor, a very honest fellow with a black beard, who uses everyone well according to his poor ability, and would use them much better if he had more of the thing the English call "means."

We set out from that city for the town commonly called Newry, which was one day's journey. There, to speak the truth, we were not very well entertained, nor according to our qualities; for that town produces nothing but lean beef, and very rarely mutton; the very worst wine; nor was there any bread, except biscuits, even in the Governor's house. However, we did our best to be merry and jocund with the bad wine, putting sugar in it (as the senior lawyers are used to do, with Canary wine)—with toasted bread, which in English is called "a lawyer's nightcap." There we found Captain Adderton, an honest fellow, and a friend of ours, who, having nothing to do, was easily persuaded to accompany us to Lecale.

So the next morning we four take horse and set out. We had no guide except Captain Caulfield, who promised he would lead us very well. But before we had ridden three miles we lost our way and were compelled to go on foot, leading our horses through bogs and marshes which were very troublesome; and some of us were not wanting who swore silently between our teeth, and wished our guide at a thousand devils. At length we came to some village of obscure name, where for two brass shillings we brought with us a countryman who might lead us to the Island of Magennis, ten miles distant from the town of Newry: for Master Morrison had promised he would meet us there.

The weather was very cold, and it began to roar dreadfully with a strong wind in our faces, when we were on the mountains, where there was neither tree nor house; but there was no remedy save patience. Captain Bodley alone had a long cloak with a hood, into which he prudently thrust his head, and laughed somewhat into himself to see the others so badly armed against the storm.

We now come to the Island of Magennis, where, alighting from our horses, we met Master Morrison and Captain Constable, with many others, whom, for the sake of brevity, I pass by. They had tarried there at least three hours, expecting our arrival, and, in the meantime, drank ale and usquebaugh with the Lady Sara, the daughter of Tyrone, and wife of the aforesaid Magennis; a truly beautiful woman: so that I can well believe these three hours did not appear to them more than a minute, especially to Master Constable, who is by nature very fond, not of women only, but likewise of dogs and horses. We also drank twice or thrice, and after we had duly kissed her, we each prepared for our journey.

It was ten or twelve miles from that island to Downpatrick, where Master Morrison dwelt; and the way seemed much longer on account of our wish to be there. At length, as all things have an end and a black pudding two (as the proverb hath it) we came by little and little to the said house. And now began that more than Lucullan entertainment, which neither Cicero, whose style in composition I chiefly imitate, (although Horace says, "O imitators! a slavish herd"), nor any other of the Latin or Greek authors, could express in suitable terms.

When we had approached within a stone's throw of the house—or rather palace—of the said Master Morrison—behold! forthwith innumerable servants! some light us with pine-wood lights and torches because it is dark; others, as soon as we alight, take our horses, and lead them into a handsome and spacious stable, where neither hay nor oats are wanting. Master Morrison himself leads us by wide stairs into a large hall where a fire is burning the height of our chins, as the saying is; and afterwards into a bed chamber, prepared in the Irish fashion.

Here having taken off our boots, we all sit down and converse on various matters; Captain Caulfield about supper and food, for he was very hungry; Captain Constable about hounds, of which he had there some excellent ones, as he himself asserted; and the rest about other things. Master Morrison ordered a cup of Spanish wine to be brought, with burnt sugar, nutmeg, and ginger, and made us all drink a good draught of it, which was very grateful to the palate, and also good for procuring an appetite for supper, if anyone needed such.

In an hour we heard some one down in the kitchen calling with a loud voice "To the Dresser." Forthwith we see a long row of servants, decently dressed, each with dishes of the most select meats, which they place on the table in the very best style. One presents to us a silver basin with the most limpid water; another hands us a very white towel; others arrange chairs and seats in their proper places. "What need of words, let us be seen in action" (as Ajax says in Ovid). Grace having been said, we begin to fix our eyes intently on the dishes, whilst handling our knives: and here you might have plainly seen those Belgian feasts, where, at the beginning is silence, in the middle the crunching of teeth, and at the end the chattering of the people. For at first we sat as if rapt and astounded by the variety of meats and dainties—like a German I once saw depicted standing between two jars, the one of white wine and the other of claret, with this motto: "I know not which way to turn."

But after a short time we fall to roundly on every dish calling now and then for wine, now and then for attendance, everyone according to his whim. In the midst of supper Master Morrison ordered be given to him a glass goblet full of claret, which measured, (as I conjecture) ten or eleven inches roundabout, and drank to the health of all, and to our happy arrival. We freely received it from him, thanking him, and drinking one after the other, as much as he drank before us. He then gave four or five healths of the chief men, and of our absent friends, just as the most illustrious Lord, now Treasurer of Ireland, is used to do at his dinners. And it is a very praiseworthy thing, and has, perhaps, more in it than anyone would believe; and there was not one amongst us who did pledge him and each other without any scruple or gainsay, which I was very glad to see; for it was a proof of unanimity and assured friendship.

For there are many (a thing I can't mention without great and extreme sorrow) who won't drink healths with others; sitting, nevertheless, in the company of those who do drink, and not doing as they do; which is of all things the most shameful.... For, at table, he who does not receive whatsoever healths may be proposed by another, does so, either because he likes not the proposer, or he to whom they drink, or the wine itself. Truly I would not willingly have any dealings with him who under values either me or my friend, or lastly wine, the most precious of all things under heaven.

••••••••••••

Let us now return to Lecale, where the supper (which, as I have said, was most elegant) being ended, we again enter our bedroom, in which was a large fire (for at the time it was exceedingly cold out of doors) and benches for sitting on; and plenty of tobacco, with nice pipes, was set before us. The wine also had begun to operate a little on us, and everyone's wits had become somewhat sharper; all were gabbling at once, and all sought a hearing at once.... Amongst other things, we said that the time was now happily different, from when we were before Kinsale at Christmas of last year, when we suffered intolerable cold, dreadful labour, and a want of almost everything; drinking the very worst. We compared events, till lately unhoped for, with the past, and with those now hoped for. Lastly, reasoning on everything, we conclude that the verse of Horace (Ode 37, Book 1st) squares exceedingly well with the present time—namely, "that now is the time for drinking, that now is the time for thumping the floor with a loose foot." Therefore, after a little Captain Jephson calls for usquebaugh, and we all immediately second him with one consent, calling out "Usquebaugh, usquebaugh"—for we could make as free there as in our own quarters.

Besides it was not without reason we drank usquebaugh; for it was the best remedy against the cold of that night, and good for dispersing the crude vapours of the French wine; and pre-eminently wholesome in these regions, where the priests themselves, who are holy men—as the Abbot of Armagh, the Bishop of Cashel, and others; and also noble men—as Henry Oge MacMahon, MacHenry—and men and women of every rank —pour usquebaugh down their throats by day and by night; and that not for hilarity only, which would be praiseworthy, but for constant drunkenness which is detestable.

Therefore, after everyone had drank two or three healths ... what because of the assailing fumes of the wine which now sought our heads ... we thought it right, as I have said, to rest for some hours. And behold, now, the great kindness that Master Morrison shows towards us. He gives up to us his own good and soft bed, and throws himself upon a pallet in the same chamber, and would not be persuaded by anything we could say, to lie in his own bed; and the pallet was very hard and thin, such as they are wont to have who are called "Palatine" of great heroes.

I need not tell how soundly we slept till morning, for that is easily understood, all things considered; at least if the old syllogism be true: "He who drinks well sleeps well." We did not, however, pass the night altogether without annoyance: for the Captain's dogs, which were very badly educated (after the Northern fashion) were always jumping on the beds, and would not let us alone, although we beat them ever so often, which the said Captain took in dudgeon, especially when he heard his dogs howling; but it was all as one for that; for it is not right that dogs, who are of the beasts, should sleep with men who are reasoning and laughing animals, according to the philosophers.... Before we get out of bed they bring to us a certain aromatic of strong ale, compounded with sugar and eggs (in English "caudle") to comfort and strengthen the stomach, they also bring beer (if any prefer it) with toasted bread and nutmeg, to allay thirst, steady the head, and cool the liver; they also bring pipes of the best tobacco to drive away rheums and catarrhs.

We now all jump quickly out of bed, put on our clothes, approach the fire, and, when all are ready, walk abroad together to take the air, which, in that region, is most salubrious and delightful, so that if I wished to enumerate all the advantages of the place, not only powers (of description), but time itself would be wanting. I shall therefore omit that, as being already known, and revert to ourselves, who, having now had a sufficient walk, returned to our lodging as dinner time was at hand. But how can we tell about the sumptuous preparation of everything? How about the dinners? How about the dainties? For we seemed as if present (as you would suppose) at the nuptial banquet to which some Cleopatra had invited her Antony; so many varieties of meat were there, so many kinds of condiments; about every one of which I would willingly say something, only that I fear being too tedious. I shall therefore demonstrate from a single dinner, what may be imagined of the rest. There was a large and beautiful collar of brawn, with its accompaniments —to wit, mustard and Muscadel wine; there were well-stuffed geese, ... the legs of which the Captain always laid hold of for himself; there were pies of venison and of various kinds of game; pasties also, some of marrow, with innumerable plums; others of it with coagulated milk; others which they call tarts, of divers shapes, materials and colours, made of beef, mutton and veal. I do not mention because they are reckoned vulgar, other kinds of dishes, wherein France much abounds, and which they designate "Quelq'choses" ["Kickshaws"]. Neither do I relate anything of the delicacies which accompanied the cheese, because they would excel all belief. I may say in one word, that all things were there supplied us most luxuriously and most copiously. And lest anyone might think that God had sent us the meat, but the Devil the Cook (as the proverb says), there was a cook there so expert in his art that his equal could scarce be found....

If you now inquire whether there were any other amusements, besides those I have related, I say an infinite number, and the very best. For if we wished to ride after dinner, you would have seen forthwith ten or twelve handsome steeds with good equipments and other ornaments, ready for the road. We quickly mount, we visit the Well and Chair of St. Patrick [Struel], the ancient Fort [Rath-Celtair], or any other place according to our fancy; and at length returning home, cards, tables, and dice are set before us, and amongst other things that Indian tobacco (of which I shall never be able to make sufficient mention), and of which I cannot speak otherwise.

••••••••••••

And now once more to our Lecale, where amongst other things that contributed to hilarity, there came one night after supper certain maskers belonging to the Irish gentry, four in number (if I rightly remember). They first sent in to us a letter marked with "the greatest haste," and "after our hearty commendations," according to the old style, saying that they were strangers, just arrived in these parts, and very desirous of spending one or two hours with us; and leave being given, they entered in this order: first a boy, with a lighted torch; then two, beating drums; then the maskers, two and two; then another torch. One of the maskers carried a dirty pocket handkerchief, with ten pounds in it, not of bullion, but of the new money lately coined, which has the harp on one side, and the royal arms on the other.

They were dressed in shirts, with many ivy leaves sewed on here and there over them; and had over their faces masks of dog-skin; with holes to see out of, and noses made of paper; their caps were high and peaked (in the Persian fashion), and were also of paper, and ornamented with the same (ivy) leaves.

I may briefly say we play at dice. At one time the drums sound on their side; at another the trumpet on ours. We fight a long time a doubtful game; at length the maskers lose, and are sent away cleaned out. Now whoever hath seen a dog, struck with a stick or a stone, run out of the house with his tail hanging between his legs, would have (so) seen these maskers going home: without money; out of spirits; out of order; without even saying "Farewell"; and they said that each of them had five or six miles to go to his home, and it was then two hours after midnight.

I shall now tell of another jest or gambol, which amongst many, the domestics of Master Morrison exhibited for us. Two servants sat down after the manner of women (with reverence be it spoken) when they "hunker," only that they (the servants) sat upon the ground: their hands were tied together in such a manner that their knees were clasped within them; and a stick placed between the bend of the arms and the legs, so that they could in no way move their arms; they held between the thumb and forefinger of either hand a small stick, almost a foot in length, and sharp at the farther end. Two are placed in this way: the one opposite the other at the distance of an ell. Being thus placed they engage; and each one tries to upset his opponent, by attacking him with his feet; for being once upset, he can by no means recover himself, but presents himself to his upsetter for attack with the aforesaid small stick. Which made us laugh so for an hour, that the tears dropped from our eyes; and the wife of Philip the cook laughed, and the scullion, who were both present. You would have said that some barber-surgeon was there to whom all were showing their teeth.

But enough of these matters; for there would be no end of writing, were I to recount all our grave and merry doings in that space of seven days.

I shall therefore make an end both of the journey and of my story. For on the seventh day from our arrival we departed, mournful and sad; and Master Morrison accompanied us as far as Dundrum; to whom each of us bid farewell, and again farewell, and shouting the same for a long way, with our caps raised above our heads, we hasten to our quarters, and there we each cogitate seriously over our own affairs.

CHAPTER V

TRADITION IN IRISH HISTORY.

Reprinted from the Nineteenth Century and After, March, 1909.

IN the *Quarterly Review* of January last there appeared an article by Mr. Robert Dunlop, dealing in a trenchant manner with a book which I wrote lately, *The Making of Ireland and Its Undoing*. I regret to take part personally in a controversy where my own credit is brought into question, and I am only moved to do so by consideration of the grave issues which are involved as regards the study of Irish history.

The appearance of my book has raised two questions of a very different order—the important question of whether, with the advance of modern studies, need has arisen for an entire review of the whole materials for Irish history and of the old conclusions, and the less interesting problem of my own inadequacy and untrustworthiness. Mr. Dunlop, in some fifteen pages of discourse, has not so much as mentioned the first. He has treated the second at considerable length. We may here take them in order of importance.

The real difference between Mr. Dunlop and myself lies deeper than the question of my merits or demerits. It is the old conflict between tradition and enquiry. For the last 300 years students of medieval Irish history have peacefully trodden a narrow track, hemmed in by barriers on either hand. On one side they have been for the most part bounded by complete ignorance of the language of the country or its literature. On the other side they have raised the wall of tradition. Along this secluded lane writers have followed one another, in the safety of the orthodox faith. A history recited with complete unanimity takes on in course of time the character of the highest truth. There have been disputes on one or two points perhaps where theologians are concerned, as for example the story of St. Patrick; but on the general current of Irish life there has been no serious discussion nor any development in opinion. The argument from universal assent has been sufficient. There is a similarity even of phrase. "We prefer to think," writes Mr. Dunlop. "We prefer to abide by the traditional view of the state of Ireland," writes another critic from the same school. Agreement has been general, individual speculation has not disturbed the peace, and all have joined their voices to swell the general creed. Under these favouring conditions historians of Ireland speak with a rare confidence and unanimity. "What are novelties after all?" cries the sagacious historian imagined by M. Anatole France: "mere impertinences."

It has happened to me to question the received doctrine. Universal assent of all men of all time is a very useful thing, and for some positive facts it may be decisive. But in Irish history it is used to enforce a series of negations—no human progress, no spiritual life, no patriotism, no development, no activity save murder, no movement but a constant falling to decay, and a doomed lapse into barbarism of every race that entered the charmed circle of the island. However universal the consent, the statements of the tradition are of so extraordinary a character, that one may fairly desire an inspection of the evidence. I have ventured to suggest that the time had come to study the sources anew; to see if any had been omitted, or if in modern research any new testimony concerning Ireland had been brought to light; to give less weight to negative assertions than to positive facts; and to enquire what the whole cumulative argument might imply. Thus the fundamental problem has been raised. If Mr. Dunlop has not a word to say about it, it will nevertheless not disappear. The enquiry will need many scholars and a long time, but I am sure it will be completed, and that Irish history will then need to be re-written. Meanwhile, as I claim no infallible authority, to fulminate against me does not get rid of the essential problem. The discrediting of a doubter of the orthodox faith is the simplest form of argument and the least laborious. The trouble is that when it is done the real question is no further advanced.

A heretic must take his risks. We have an example of their gravity in this article, in which Mr. Dunlop restores an old custom to controversy. We had almost come to suppose that it was the privilege of theologians to settle the respective platforms from which disputations should be carried on. The higher plane is reserved for the orthodox. The "querulous" dissentient, on the other hand, is pronounced to be making mere incursions into what is for him a comparatively unknown region, his incapacity is obvious and his want of candour deplorable, and he has forfeited all claim to respect. This is all in the appropriate manner of those who hold an Irish history handed down by tradition.

The permitted belief about Ireland has been summed up dogmatically by Mr. Dunlop in the *Dictionary of National Biography*, the *Cambridge Modern History*, and elsewhere. Of the inhabitants of Ireland "two-thirds at least led a wild and half nomadic existence. Possessing no sense of national unity beyond the narrow limits of the several clans to which they belonged, acknowledging no law outside the customs of their tribe, subsisting almost entirely on the produce of their herds and the spoils of the chase, and finding in their large frieze mantles a sufficient protection against the inclemency of the weather, and one relieving them from the necessity of building houses for themselves, they had little in their general mode of life to distinguish them from their Celtic ancestors." "Outside the pale there was nothing worthy of being called a Church. To say that the Irish had relapsed into a state of heathenism is perhaps going too far. The tradition of a Christian belief still survived; but it was a lifeless, useless thing." The country was "cut off by its position, but even more by the relapse of the greater of its inhabitants into a state of semi-barbarism, from the general currents of European development." Bogs and woods, the lairs of the wild-boar and the wolf, made internal communications dangerous and difficult, and prevented trade and intercourse with other nations. Few words, therefore, are needed to sum up their commerce. "French wines found their way into the country through Cork and Waterford; the long-established relations between Dublin and Bristol still subsisted; Spanish traders landed their wares on Galway quay; the fame of St. Patrick's purgatory attracted an occasional pilgrim from foreign lands; and of one Irish chieftain it was placed on record that he had accomplished the hazardous journey to Rome and back." Shane O'Neill, "champion of Celtic civilisation," could speak no language but Irish, and could not sign his name. In the *Quarterly Review* we have a few more details—that the main part of the Irishmen's dress was skins; that this people who lived without houses when they went on their "marauding expeditions" (excursions of the full summer time) made to themselves tents of untanned skins to cover them (here I could almost imagine Mr. Dunlop, in spite of his aversion to bards, indulging on the sly in a cloudy reminiscence of an Irish poet); that among the whole of them they had just a few hundred coracles made of osiers and skins for crossing swollen rivers, for the O'Malleys and O'Driscolls who had long-boats represented "perhaps the Iberian element in the *nation*," suggests Mr. Dunlop, not to give the Gaels any credit, while he slips by the way into the objectionable word apparently so hard to avoid; that they made no practical use even of their inland fisheries, and had no industries, so that even the cloth was made by Englishmen.

We would desire to ask Mr. Dunlop for the exact proof he relies on for any one of these statements, beginning perhaps with "no law outside the *customs of the tribe*." Writers who hold Ireland to be, as he says, "a sort of scrap-heap for Europe," and who cannot conceive of medieval Irishmen as ordinary men sharing the faults and virtues of other white Europeans, are addicted to the word "native"—a word not in common use among historians for Englishmen in England in the Middle Ages, but affected by them to indicate Irishmen in Ireland, with the derogatory sense which their "tradition" requires. The vulgar view received as it were official recognition half a century ago from Mr. Hamilton in his preface to the *State Papers* of 1509-73 (see also references in my book, 487-8), where he explains that the study of Irish life till Elizabethan times will be of considerable value in the study of *Universal History*, Ireland being so remote from the earlier seats of civilisation that the rude way of living described by Hesiod and the old poets still lingered there till the sixteenth century; till which time "most of the wild Irish led a nomade life, tending cattle, sowing little corn, and rarely building houses, but sheltered alike from heat and cold, and moist and dry, by the Irish cloak." The last fifty years, we see, amid the general shaking of dry bones and the movement of history elsewhere, have brought no stir in Irish history. That alone stands like eternal truth fixed and unchangeable. Hence, doubtless, Mr. Dunlop's canon (*Quart. Rev.*, 1906) forbidding "*a history of Ireland in more than one volume*."

The barbarian legend has got a long start. A first attempt to review its evidence was made in my book. In a series of social studies I have endeavoured to discuss, not the whole of Irish history, but definite matters of trade, social life, and education. I have gathered a body of facts which indicate that Ireland had considerable manufactures; that her foreign commerce can be traced throughout Europe; that there was an orderly society, even a wealthy one; that Irish travellers were known at Rome and in the Levant; that there was an Anglo-Irish culture by no means contemptible, in touch with Continental learning; and that increasing intercourse of the races did not tend to barbarism but to civilisation.

In this sketch I have not proposed to myself to draw nice distinctions between what the Normans precisely did, and what the Irish (or even, following Mr. Dunlop), what Iberians were doing in the sixteenth century in the joint work of commerce and culture, because there is as yet no sufficient material for that discussion; I share this lack of knowledge with many who have pronounced themselves with no uncertain voice. Further, I should have been glad to confine these studies to the cheerful progress of trade and culture; but I was confronted with two possible objections. The suggestion that if there had been any considerable trade it would not have vanished by a freak, could only be answered by indicating how and why the destruction had been wrought. And to meet the argument that historians would not have let a genuine story perish, I gave my opinion on how it was that the truth dropped out of sight.

My conclusions conflict with the venerable traditions over which Mr. Dunlop mounts guard. I clearly offend also against the canon of one volume. It is obvious that he must feel for me the sharpest disapproval; and this censure is conveyed with no mitigation of phrase or manner.

The charge he elaborates against me is briefly that I have no judgment, and less candour, in the use of documents, and have thus produced a mass of mischievous fiction.

I may say in passing that Mr. Dunlop's severity with regard to authorities comes somewhat oddly from one who has shown himself fairly easy in such matters. In his own writings he gives no references, and in this same article the only authority he quotes independently is Mr. O'Connor's *Elizabethan Ireland.* When I have to be silenced, "Turn we to Mr. O'Connor!" Now Mr. O'Connor has written a slight sketch of Irish political and social life in some 280 pages. He gives no dates, no indications of place, and no references. But we have Mr. Dunlop's word for it that it is a "scholarly" work. "Mr. O'Connor" quoted by Mr. Dunlop ends controversy. The tradition is secure. I might envy Mr. Dunlop this freedom from trammels of references, of date, or of place. In such wide and impartial survey any statement about Ireland may appear as true of every place and of all time. Barbarism would seem to be a fixed and unchanging state, a passive monotony, from the time of "Lacustrine habitations" and of "Hesiod and the old poets," till its characteristic representative in Shane O'Neill. The principle once assumed, any evidence will suffice to show that the Irish had none of the attributes of ordinary white Europeans; while evidence that they made money, traded, built houses, talked Latin, studied medicine and law, or otherwise behaved like other people of the Middle Ages, is probably rhodomontade, moonshine, or historical profligacy.

Mr. Dunlop's summary method with unfamiliar sources appears in his asperity towards what he calls my "trivial references" to Mr. Standish Hayes O'Grady's*Catalogue of Manuscripts*.

"We wonder (he says on p. 267) how many of Mrs. Green's readers are aware that of this book, from which she has gleaned so much information —of a sort—only one copy, so far as we know, is accessible to the public, and that is in the MSS. Department of the British Museum. The book, we understand, was never published. It is still incomplete. The official copy consists merely of the bound sheets as they were printed off for proof."

I suppose Mr. Dunlop does not mean to suggest that the value of a book is in proportion to the number of copies, or that an authority of which a single copy exists should not be quoted. In any case I can reassure him. The sheets of this *Catalogue* have been these many years past for sale to the public at the Museum, where I got my copy, and I hope many others did the same. The book can be bought in a London shop to-day. Mr. Dunlop might consult it in the London Library. The copy placed in the National Library in Dublin in 1895 has been in frequent use since then. Possibly Mr. Dunlop knows the inside of the book better than the outside, but it seems to be a new acquaintance, suddenly introduced and viewed with distaste. In this brilliant *Catalogue*we have the work of a very great authority, unsurpassed in his special learning, far beyond what

O'Donovan could lay claim to; with its "information—of a sort—" it is the most important book that has appeared for many years with regard to Irish history. Another critic of Mr. Dunlop's school, who in his remarks gives no definite sign of any knowledge of Mr. O'Grady's work, has reproached me for referring to it "without further sifting." But it is certain that neither of these writers who reprove me will themselves do much "further sifting" where that admirable scholar has gone before them.

May I add that Mr. Dunlop does not appear to follow too closely modern studies on Irish affairs, or he would surely have known of Mr. Justice Madden's *Classical Learning in Ireland*, published last summer—a little book which he should certainly have been willing to include in any review of recent Irish writings?

To return, however, to my own lamentable want of candour and accuracy, I now give a few of the instances of my deficiencies, and of the admirable example which Mr. Dunlop sets me in these respects.

Mr. Dunlop states, "to speak accurately," that my reference to Shane O'Neill as "done to death" (so *he* expresses it) by the English is "absolutely without foundation." His own account of Shane's death in the *Dictionary of National Biography* tells us that "possibly if he could have kept a civil tongue in his head the MacDonnells might have consented to a reconciliation." "It is doubtful whether his assassination was premeditated ... it is probable that when heated with wine he may have irritated them by his insolent behaviour beyond endurance." In the *Cambridge Modern History* (iii. 592), however, Mr. Dunlop has attained conviction. "In his wine-cups," he tells us, "he began to brawl, and was literally hacked in pieces by his enemies." These and some other of his suppositions do not appear to agree with the story in *Holinshed, Campion, the Calendar of State Papers*, or the *Four Masters*. But why does Mr. Dunlop disagree with Lord Deputy Sidney, the main mover in the matter? Many efforts, it is well known, had been made to murder Shane. In 1566 Sidney sent to Scotland his "man," the English-Scot Douglas, who had come to him from Leicester himself. Sidney gives us the clue to his mission. "I pray you," he wrote to

Leicester, "let this bringer (Douglas) receive comfortable words of you. I have found him faithful, *it was he that brought the Scots that killed O'Neill.*" Douglas repeated the boast and prayed a reward from Cecil. Years later Sidney, being maligned by powerful enemies at Court, reminded the Queen of his old services. "And whereas he [O'Neill] looked for service at their [the Scots] hands against me, *for service of me, they killed him....* But when I came to the Court," he added with indignation, "it was told me it was no war that I had made, nor worthy to be called a war, for that Shane O'Neill was but a beggar, an outlaw, and one of no force, and *that the Scots stumbled on him by chance*." Would Mr. Dunlop, as a means of overthrowing me, join with Sidney's enemies to rob him of the deed he boasted of? (*Vide Sid. Let.* 12, 34-5; *C.S.P.* i. 430; *Car.* ii. 338, 340-1.)

I have pained Mr. Dunlop by referring to the hoard of Con O'Neill, Earl of Tyrone, as evidence that Ulster was not penniless. Mr. Dunlop discovers that Shane O'Neill "robbed his father" of this store, and can scarcely believe that I adduce this "robbery" to prove the wealth of Ulster, and that I use it in connection with a passage about plunder of Ireland by English invaders. This hoard occurs in a list of three pages containing signs of riches in Ireland (pp. 67-69), a mere glance at which would show the absurdity of any contention that all the moneys I mention fell into English hands. As to Con O'Neill's savings, I see no objection to an allusion to them as one proof among others of money and plate in Ulster. I do not know if Mr. Dunlop means not only to suggest my want of candour, but also to prove that if Shane "robbed" his father's treasure, therefore no English soldiers or officials robbed any Irish chief of his plate or wealth.

But though in this connection I have really nothing to do with the ultimate fate of Con's hoard, I may in passing compare the Lord Chancellor Cusack's report at the time with Mr. Dunlop's "robbery." Con O'Neill was thrown into prison in Dublin in 1552, and said to be threatened with death. The English were prepared with an illegitimate successor in Tyrone. Shane claimed to be his father's lawful heir, and fought the English nominee. A garrison of English soldiers was thrown into Armagh. Beyond the Blackwater Ford, within a ride of Armagh, lay the chief fort of Tyrone, on the great hill of Dungannon. Shane, evidently with the support of his people, "came to Dungannon," and took with him "of the chief's treasure £800 in gold and silver besides plate and other stuff" [apparently then not the whole of it, but so much as was needed for the war at the moment] "and retaineth the same as yet, whereby it appeareth that he and she [the Earl and Countess] was content with the same; for," said Cusack, "it could not be perceived that they were greatly offended for the same." This was how Shane O'Neill "robbed his father."

Mr. Dunlop quotes a sentence that "Galway ships sailed to Orkney and to Lübeck," and gives *one* only of my references in the note, which states that a Scottish ship of Orkney was freighted at Galway for Lisbon. It is evident that by one of the accidental errors of transcription, which every writer that ever lived has sometimes to deplore, I transferred the words, and *Orkney* was used where I meant to write *Lisbon*. Lübeck is a different matter. Why did Mr. Dunlop carefully omit the reference in the same note to the page where I mention goods shipped from Galway to Lübeck in 1416? Was it a generous effort to make the error take on a more serious character? Or was it a common inaccuracy? I may inform him that in the *Hansisches Urkundenbuch* further references occur to Irish cloth at Lübeck, as well as to Irish cloth and provisions along the Elbe, and that the name he throws doubt on appears with good reason in my text.

Mr. Dunlop also discovers a "most apparent and painful" instance of my "distorting of evidence" in my reference (which I did not give as a quotation) to Limerick merchants appeached of treason for *trading* with Irish rebels, when the deputy's words were *victualling and maintaining* (p. 170). Mr. Dunlop might perhaps himself suspect some barter in the business when it attracted eight merchants to traffic in so dangerous an enterprise. But he conveniently omits the rest of my story, that within a year of the arrest of the eight merchants the Limerick corporation prayed to have the city charter confirmed with a special clause *that they might buy and sell with Irishmen at all times*. They seem to have had no objection to trade with the Irish, which was the only point I had there to prove. I willingly alter the word that seems to Mr. Dunlop so painful a distortion of the truth, and my argument remains unchanged.

Mr. Dunlop twice condemns me in "the case of Enniscorthy fair, where the documents referred to refute the deduction drawn from them." "We strongly resent her concealing the fact" that Sidney, with the Four Masters, deplored the "*destruction*(n.b.)" of the fair by the rebellious Butlers at the instigation of James Fitzmaurice. Why should I not "conceal facts" I do not know to be true? I fancy it is better than publishing them. The word used by the Four Masters, Sidney, and a contemporary letter given in Hore's *Town of Wexford* (175) is "spoiling." Will Mr. Dunlop give his references to "*destruction* (n.b.)," and to "the instigation of James Fitzmaurice"? What is the proof? This day's raid was not the first attack on the fair after it had been granted to English officers charged to execute martial law on the Wexford Irish. I have not space to tell the significant circumstances. Mr. Dunlop blames me for not giving the founder of the fair. "We will overlook the omission," he says in his lofty way of superior erudition and fidelity to facts. This cheap taunt is surely absolutely unworthy of a writer who should be aware that no one as yet knows the origin of the fair. I see no reason against mentioning its existence, among many others which Mr. Dunlop neglects, as evidence of trading activity in a region where Irish law and speech prevailed.

I do not propose to weary the reader by multiplying instances of this kind. The details of historical controversy interest few readers. Its personal aspect should interest none. The instances I have given are true samples of all the rest. I have gone carefully through the long indictment, and I note half a dozen minor points in which I am glad to correct an obvious misprint or to amend an error (not one of which, I would say, affects the drift of my argument). But the great bulk of these criticisms—grave inaccuracies in themselves, or misstatements of what I say, or dogmatic assertions which need for their discussion evidences which there is no attempt to offer—can give me little help. For an example of historical investigation of medieval Irish history, of serious use of references and evidences, or of customary fairness in discussion, I must go elsewhere than to Mr. Dunlop.

With regard to evidence, I am charged with repudiating the testimony of Spenser, Davies, Fynes Moryson, Cuellar, Derrick, and official documents that tell against me. I have drawn very largely from State Papers and official records of all kinds, sources of information which have proved invaluable for my purpose. In the shaking bog of medieval testimony, some firm standing is to be found in statutes, ordinances, town records, cartularies, and the like. From them we rapidly come to more perilous regions—State Papers and letters—where every document needs to be considered as a separate "source" to be separately discussed. Some were written by strangers newly come to the country—soldiers, secretaries, adventurers, spies; others by higher officials struggling in an intricate tangle of intrigues, or by a lower sort trying to make their way upwards; some by governors zealous to keep their credit amid the scandal of the Court; others by governors desperate to recapture a lost reputation. In the medley of partiality, prejudice, ignorance, despair, and triumph, every one must judge to the best of his ability as to the value of the testimony; there can be no scientific accuracy in the measurement. There is the same difficulty with the reports of a few Continental travellers, Italian or Spanish. Historians of Ireland have freely used the evidence of men, English or European, who came not knowing a word of the language, who traversed the country more or less rapidly under official guidance, or in the midst of armies occupied in a peculiarly ferocious warfare, or who attempted an uneasy living on the confiscated lands of the "native" people—men, in fact, who knew practically nothing but destruction. From the study of other evidence I have come to think that the view which has generally been accepted from these gentlemen is imperfect and often erroneous. They could know nothing of an earlier time and had but a partial vision of their own.

Some well-thumbed later authorities have been found to give no trustworthy guidance for medieval Ireland, and they do not appear in that customary place of authority which had become their recognised privilege; on the other hand, some entirely new authorities have been called in and some have lain unused.

Among the writers I am accused of neglecting is Captain Cuellar, a Spaniard from the Armada, knowing no Irish, flying for his life, sometimes among people who had no good reputation with the Irish themselves, hiding himself in the wildest and most secret haunts of districts swept and wasted from end to end by English soldiers—I do not know why such an experience should be quoted as a fair record of ordinary Irish life in the plains, in times of peace, and among the richer and more settled clans. Mr. Orpen, in the *English Historical Review*, has extracted from this little record every damaging phrase to the Irish to be found in it and omitted every favourable one. Does he wonder why I have not done the like? I have not done it because I do not think it fair dealing or honest history to state as evidence against the Irish that Cuellar was "robbed of all he possessed, stripped naked, beaten, and forced by a blacksmith to work"; and not to mention that the robbing and beating was the work of English troops and mercenaries from Scotland; that the week he spent at the blacksmith's forge was the solitary unkindness he suffered from any native Irishman in his seven months' wandering; that the moment an Irish chief heard of his misfortune he sent to take him to his own house; that in that seven months of journeyings in the wilds, from the day when cast on a Connacht beach, he was hidden in pity by gallow-glasses till the day when men of Ulster secured his escape across the sea, he was continually succoured by young and old, men and women, clerics and laymen, who pitied him, wept at his sufferings, showed him every hospitality and kindness, and guided him from shelter to shelter to hide him from the English. By what strange tradition, by what long prejudice is this perversion of evidence fabricated and admitted?

Besides English and Spanish testimony we have also some from the Irish themselves. Among Irish witnesses the great Galway scholar Dr. Lynch, writer of *Cambrensis Eversus*, stands high; no student can afford to neglect editions and translations made by Mr. Whitley Stokes and Professor Kuno Meyer in this country, and by Continental scholars; the translations of Dr. Douglas Hyde; the work of Dr. Norman Moore in the *Dictionary of National Biography* and elsewhere; or the collection of criticisms, translations, and summaries that make up the invaluable *Catalogue of Manuscripts* in the British Museum by Mr. S. H. O'Grady.

Mr. Dunlop does not like poets. "Surely she must know that the very stock-in-trade of a poet is pure moonshine," he avers. However that may be, I may say that Mr. O'Grady's *Catalogue* contains a great deal that is not poetry. "Must we remind her," says Mr. Dunlop with the loftiest severity, "that bard and annalist were often the same individual?" The *Catalogue* would explain to him how impossible would be such a conception to the Irish world, where a bard was a mere natural poet who had not studied in the schools. Will Mr. Dunlop give one single instance of this frequent fact? A quotation from a blind poet peculiarly awakens his contempt, as he refers to it twice, repeating here the criticism of another writer of his school. Teigue Dall O'Higgin was a man of great eminence in his day; and I see no reason to believe that a blind man necessarily takes leave of *all* his senses. I have no doubt that Teigue was at home in all the gossip of Enniskillen, and that he could distinguish between the sounds of a smith's shop, or of women talking over their embroidery, and of men bringing boats to the shore. Other references to Fermanagh which I have given in my book, and indications in the English wars of the importance of water carriage on the lake, bear out the story of Teigue the Blind. He was right about the "blue hills."

If Mr. Dunlop accuses me of a "partiality for native records" with all their "rhetorical rhodomontade," I frankly confess to a regard for the opinion of people who belong to a country and speak its tongue. I suppose that contemporary Irish witnesses, even the *Four Masters*, may be used with the same authority and the same limitations as English; nor do I know why the opinion of any stray traveller or minor official from over-sea, intent only on furthering his interests, is to be accepted without question, while the word of a deeply learned Anglo-Irish scholar of Galway, or of an eminent Irish poet who had visited every province of Ireland, is to be wholly suspect. I will give an illustration by recalling the case of Sir John Davies and of Dr. Lynch. To Mr. Dunlop the brief writings of Davies represent a very high authority, while the*Cambrensis Eversus* of Lynch is dismissed in one word as a "political pamphlet." He does not apparently think Davies had any political leanings. We usually think people impartial who hold our own opinions.

In my book I have given definite reasons for thinking that Davies' acquaintance with Irish affairs was inadequate—in a short residence in the country of which he did not know the language, the law, or the history. My own judgment is that considering his imperfect means of knowledge, and his very strong bias of prejudice, his statements about Ireland before his coming there have no particular sanctity, and need to be tested and corroborated like those of any other writer. That he is sometimes at fault even a believer such as Mr. Dunlop seems in a hidden way to admit. Suggesting that my references to the cloth trade are not so novel as unwary readers might think, "the excellent quality of Irish wool," says Mr. Dunlop, "is one of the best attested facts in Irish commercial history." Then why has Mr. Dunlop until this moment excluded any slightest mention of wool in his summary of Irish trade? Was it too well known? Or was it because of the saying of Sir John Davies—"for wool and wool-felts were ever of little value in this kingdom?" We are here shut into a denial of the well-attested commerce in wool, or to a doubt of the sufficiency of Sir John Davies as a witness; and we are left without guidance by Mr. Dunlop. On the whole, it seems judicious to depend on Davies' evidence only for the things that lay within his immediate and direct observation. His opinion on all that he himself saw is worthy of respect, and we may admit the sound legal maxim that a man's evidence can always be accepted when it is given against himself.

The same distinction may surely be drawn in the case of Dr. Lynch. Davies was a man of English and Latin learning, Lynch a man of Irish and Latin learning. The historical criticism of their day was not perfect in either country, and as Davies leant to the English side of prejudice, Lynch leant to the Irish. But Lynch, like Davies, was I believe a just reporter of what he had himself seen or had heard from firsthand witnesses. And I have therefore quoted him, as I have Davies, for what had come within the range of his personal knowledge, not for matters of historical research. His testimony is of extraordinary and pathetic interest. Born in Galway in the last years of Elizabeth, when the city still preserved its old culture and the remnants of its old wealth, Lynch was one of the last scholars who ever saw and knew the Anglo-Irish civilisation. It is not any single picture that he gives that is important; it is the host of scattered and chance allusions, as to things well known to every Irishman in his day, which reveal to us the society in which he had been brought up. It is touching to remember that he was the last to say a good word for the medieval civilisation. After his death a darkness and silence of hundreds of years fell over that story, and it is across nearly three centuries that Irishmen will now have to take hands with Lynch and carry on his justification of the Ireland which was being gradually built up by the work of Gaels, Danes, Normans, and English in their common country.

This, however, is just what Mr. Dunlop denies. He "begs leave to doubt" that the "native Irish" in the fifteenth century developed the resources of the country. By omitting all contemporary references to timber, to leather, and to salmon, of course it can be said there was no medieval trade in these. The plan seems unsatisfactory, and I have not followed it. Mr. Dunlop, for example, blames me for not quoting an English poem (no pure moonshine here—perhaps a farthing dip) which does not mention leather, as proof that there was no leather trade. I have quoted the *Libel* elsewhere, but on this point I preferred the direct evidence of the records of the Bruges Staple; and I have since added notices in the *Hansisches Urkundenbuch* for leather sent in 1304, 1327, 1453 to Bruges, Dinant, and Portugal. I would ask which is the historical method: to close the question once for all with the negative silence of an anonymous English writer "whom we think," says Mr. Dunlop, in one of his easy moods about evidence, "had a pretty accurate notion of what constituted Irish commerce"; or to pursue enquiry in business records of the ports and seek to ascertain the exact facts.

The art of making linen was known, according to Mr. Dunlop, to the "native Irish, as it is to most primitive races." But what they made in Ireland was "of a very coarse kind, and its use was practically restricted to the wealthier class—viz., the merchants of the towns." What is his proof for all this? Was it the town merchants that Campion describes wearing linen shirts for wantonness and bravery, "thirty yards are little enough for one of them"? What about the great linen rolls on the Irishwomen's heads, and (is the inference too romantic?) perhaps on their bodies also? What about the fine linen in which the Galway women wrapped the Spanish hanged after the Armada? When I read of 6000 bales of linen cloth sent from Galway to Genoa in 1492, or of 4000 linen cloths mentioned in 1499 in another Galway merchant's will, or of the "sardok" of mixed woollen and linen in the Netherland markets in 1353, or of Henry the Eighth forbidding Galway any more to export linen, the records of the time seem to conflict with the opinions which Mr. Dunlop "begs leave" to hold.

Mr. Dunlop now admits for the first time some trade in cloth, but with a stipulation of his own that it was all made by Englishmen. He does not trouble to consider such a clue as we find in the State Papers of Galway merchants carrying their wine into the country to exchange among other things for cloth. He has his own theory; "it is pretty clear from such expressions as Limerick cloak, Galway mantle, Waterford rug, that the centres of the cloth industry lay within the sphere of English influence"; the participation of the Irish was excluded by severe guild regulations, and "it may not be unfair to infer that the reputation acquired abroad by Ireland in regard to its serges was not due to the industry of its native population." This insinuating hypothesis is a flaming fact on the next page, where it appears the "native Irish" (no inferring here to dull the conclusion) "took no part in the commercial development of their country, leaving it to the stranger within their gate, and thereby earning from the latter the reproach of idleness." If there were, as Mr. Dunlop "prefers to think," some loyal Irishmen who preferred English civilisation and the chances it offered them of pushing their way in life to their native customs, he states that the presence even of such loyal Irishmen "was not always welcome to citizens of English blood." Thus the English of the towns must have toiled day and night to supply the mantles which the English Government forbade to loyal people, and to provide cloaks and cloth for the foreign trade, since in their incessant struggle to preserve themselves intact from Celtic influences they refused the aid of Irish hands to work for them. It is an idyllic picture of high purpose and endeavour, of the way to develop a country, and to make an empire.

We are not, however, shut up to this series of hypotheses. The town records themselves and English State Papers, as I have shown, give sufficient proof that the "native population" were not, in fact, rejected from the town industries. Mr. Dunlop denies this; he thinks the towns remained pure English. He is sure that all the Galway people shaved their upper lip weekly. Henry the Eighth was not so sure of it when, in 1536, he sent orders from Westminster to Galway men to shave themselves aright. When Mr. Dunlop, to prove that the Galway citizens consistently desired to keep themselves free from Irish customs, quotes laws against Irish games and keening, he quotes them without date. My contention is that, if it was necessary *as late as 1527 and 1625* to enact these laws, this, with a number of other indications that I have mentioned, shows that the citizens' "desire" was not very effective, and that there was an Irish population ready to push its way in trade, but not anxious to drop "their native customs." No doubt the extent to which Irish names were changed must be conjectural; but there is evidence that such change did take place. My suggestion that "White" may indicate an Irish house gives Mr. Dunlop an opportunity to parade his knowledge of Gaelic. He informs me, on the authority of O'Donovan, that there is no such Gaelic name as *Geal* and imagines that settles the matter. He has never, then, heard of the name *Fionn*, which has been anglicised by "White" for centuries, just as a well-known Scotch writer of our day calls himself Henry White or Fionn indifferently.

As for intellectual culture, Mr. Dunlop is brevity itself. He has scarce a page for that chimera. The Irish were barbarous and the Anglo-Normans contaminated. His method is summary. The evidence of Mr. Whitley Stokes, of Dr. Norman Moore, of Mr. S. H. O'Grady, of Dr. Kuno Meyer has too little importance with him to be mentioned, and he can thus more easily avoid all proof of Irish scientific skill in medicine, or of the admirable quality of their translations from the Latin. He necessarily omits all mention of the many Irish scholars on the Continent, for has he not himself told us only one Irish chieftain made the perilous journey to Rome and back? He has no reference to buildings or arts which indicate the intercourse of Irish chiefs with the Continent. He is silent on the schools from which Irishmen were able to pass to foreign universities. He seems not to have heard of evidence of Latin culture collected by Mr.

Justice Madden. And most wonderful to say, he seems entirely unaware of the importance of the list I have published, for the first time (by the generous kindness of a great scholar), of Irish translations of Continental works. Perhaps he felt himself anticipated by the conclusive comment I saw from a dashing newspaper critic, that "the Irish evidently satisfied themselves with translations!" In any case, he never hints at this list or its value as evidence. So astonishing a neglect of the greater matters of evidence, while every detail that could by any means discredit me is searched out, is surely a grave abuse of the historical method. In the matter of culture Mr. Dunlop confines himself with a singular restraint to a single topic—the list of Irishmen at Oxford. In this he counts many Anglo-Norman and only seventeen Gaelic names, and this solitary fact is enough to make him astonished that I "did not recognise how utterly untenable is her theory of the absorption of Anglo-Irish culture by the native Irish." Those readers who will turn to the chapters on Irish learning in my book will perhaps be astonished not at the theory that there was culture in Ireland, but at the travesty of that theory and the suppression of evidence which serves as historical criticism for Mr. Dunlop.

Mr. Dunlop meets with a direct negative my statement that Sussex and Sidney carried off in their train every notable chief's son they could lay hands on, but he gives no more than his own authority. My statement is perhaps too comprehensive, but I have given numerous instances (pp. 425-437) to show that the method certainly used by Sussex and Sidney, so far as they could, was steadily increased and extended in proportion as the English power gradually spread over one Irish region after another. The English took over the Irish system of hostages, but they developed it in a new way. The Catholic chief's son was brought up in London as a Protestant, in English law and language and tradition, with the avowed purpose of spiritually severing him from his people, and leaving the clan without a natural leader or defender in the national conflict; their chiefs, in fact, were to be made the very instruments for dividing and subjugating their own people. In the words I quoted, it was a method which "not only rent asunder the bonds of national loyalty and of natural affection, but which forced parent and child alike to believe that in this world and in the world to come they were divided by an impassable abyss." Surely there is no likeness in this deliberate plan to the Irish chief's use of his hostage; it was, indeed, practised with consummate art by Turkey.

In this article Mr. Dunlop proposed to prove two facts: first, that Celtic civilisation is largely a figment of my imagination; and, secondly, that far from composing one nation, the English element in Ireland was proud of its origin, and struggled incessantly to preserve itself intact from Celtic influence. One part of his plan is destructive, and the second constructive. Unfortunately the work of destruction has proved so alluring that the constructive scheme is abandoned. As to the value of the destructive work, I contend that Mr. Dunlop's criticisms are not so historically accurate, so reasonable, or so candid, that they can serve for correction or instruction. I contend further that even on the generous assumption that the whole of Mr. Dunlop's criticisms might happen to be valid, there would still remain untouched the main body of my evidence and the whole current of my argument. And I confidently believe that the history of Ireland will be re-written on truer lines and surer foundations than those sketched out in the *Cambridge Modern History* and the *Quarterly Review*. But perhaps Mr. Dunlop will go farther. It would be pleasant to hear, in more detail, his views on "the Iberian element in the nation."

Printed in Great Britain
by Amazon

55433914R00076